Learn Python Quickly

A Complete Beginner's Guide to Learning Python, Even If You're New to Programming

{CodeQuickly}

CodeQuickly.org

Free Bonus + Source Code

Programming can be hard if you don't avoid these 7 biggest mistakes! Visit codequickly.org/bonus to get this free PDF guide, and gain access to the source code for this book.

codequickly.org/bonus

Table of Contents

This page intentionally left blank.

Foreword

Python is one of the most popular programming languages in the world right now, and it's getting more popular all the time. It is powerful, robust, easy to use, and combines a diverse toolkit with intuitive syntax. Given these attributes, it's no wonder that Python has become so widely used. However, learning Python isn't necessarily simple. Just like learning any language, there's a lot to learn when it comes to Python, and it can be hard to know exactly where to start. Beyond that, after you've learned Python's syntax, how do you start completing your own projects? And how do you move from a beginner to an intermediate Python programmer? It can be intimidating just to be handed a set of tools and be expected to use them without any guidance. Don't worry, we will show you how to use the tools you learn about through structured exercises and two projects at the very end.

This book will take you through Python in a step-by-step manner, teaching you the basics and building on those basics to move towards more advanced topics. We begin by covering the basics of Python syntax, such as variables, operators, data types, and data structures. After this, we move on to intermediate topics like functions, modules, and object-oriented programming. After covering these topics, the book will go into some advanced Python techniques, including recursion, image manipulation, and unit testing. We'll also spend some time looking at how to use some of the many open-source Python libraries that are available. Finally, the last portion of the book covers two different Python programming projects you can work on to see how all the concepts you've learned come together.

The first project is a story idea generator that will help you understand how to manipulate text and reinforce basic programming principles you learned. The second project is a more challenging weather application that will help you learn how to work with outside data (in this case, data from the Internet), manipulate it, and present it in a user-friendly format. It's essential to know how to collect data from the outside world and integrate it into your programs. This is often the most exciting part of programming.

Python is an excellent language to learn for both first-time programmers and expert programmers who are looking to expand their existing skillset. Python's intuitive syntax makes it easy to use and learn, so it's a good language for first-time programmers to pick up. Despite this, Python is also flexible and extremely powerful, making it well-suited for advanced programmers as well. In fact, Python is used for everything, from mobile app development to DevOps to machine learning and artificial intelligence. Learning Python will dramatically increase the types of jobs you'll be able to apply to and be successful in. This is part of the reason I'm so passionate about helping others learn Python. It gives you access to all kinds of new techniques and tools that can improve your life in a variety of ways.

If you'd like, Python can also help you automate many repetitive tasks you face in your life, saving you a great deal of time and energy. Do you need to fill in a spreadsheet with data from multiple work emails? Python can automate that process, making it quick and easy. Would you like to create your own website where you can host your content? Python can help you do that as well, letting you make highly customizable yet elegant webpages. Do you want to analyze data and learn about the world around you? Python happens to be one of the most widely used languages for data science. If you'd like, you can also learn how to implement machine learning with Python, which will open doors to AI.

For all the reasons covered above and more, Python is a fantastic language to learn, and this book will help you go from zero knowledge of Python to a skilled Python programmer. It will provide you with the knowledge you need to start creating your own Python projects and applications successfully. It's worth noting that this book alone won't make you a Python master; you'll also need to spend time exploring and developing Python code by yourself. Not only will you need discipline, but you'll also need to know where to find additional Python resources. However, this book will give you the fundamentals necessary to start working with more advanced Python concepts. You'll be set on the path to becoming a true and effective Python developer, and you'll be able to start exploring on your own, map in hand.

If you're ready to get started, turn the page and dive in.

Chapter 1:
Introducing Python

1.1 - What is Python?

Python, created in 1990 by Guido van Rossu, is a general-purpose, high-level programming language. It has become extremely popular over the past decade, thanks to its intuitive nature, flexibility, and versatility. Python can be used on a wide variety of operating systems, and its clean, readable code style makes it relatively beginner-friendly. While not as fast as other languages, such as C++ or Java, Python code is often much shorter and simpler than other languages.

Python also supports several packages and modules created by other developers to make the development of Python applications quicker and easier.

1.2 - Why Learn Python?

There are hundreds of different programming languages out there in the world, with Wikipedia listing over 700 notable languages. Given how many languages you could potentially learn, why learn Python?

Python has seen an explosion in popularity in recent years, driven by several aspects that make it an incredibly versatile and intuitive language. A huge selling point of Python is the cleanliness and readability of its syntax and structure. Commands in Python can often be carried out using simple English keywords, which makes the language much more intuitive than many other languages. Python is also quite versatile in the sense that it supports both structured programming and object-oriented programming approaches. Python even allows the use of certain aspects of functional programming.

Python is supported by many different operating systems, including Windows, Mac, and Linux platforms. Since Python is an interpreted programming language, Python programs can run on multiple platforms without being recompiled.

Python comes with a robust standard library of modules, functions, and tools. Every module that comes with Python is a powerful tool you can use without developing additional code. Python comes pre-packaged with modules that assist in the creation of various web services, manipulating strings, and working with the operating system's interface. Python also makes it easy for users to create libraries and frameworks, meaning that there is a large, open-source Python community continually creating a wide variety of applications. Utilizing these open-source applications can significantly speed up and simplify the development of your own application.

Despite its simplicity, Python is also sturdy and robust enough to carry out complex scientific and mathematical tasks. Python has been designed with features that drastically simplify the visualization and analysis of data, making Python the go-to choice for the creation of machine learning models and artificial intelligence (AI).

For all these reasons, Python is one of the fastest-growing and most in-demand computer programming skills.

1.3 - A Note on Python Versions

There are various versions of Python available. It is highly recommended that you use version 3.7 or later when following along with this book. While Python 2 remains popular in some communities, support for Python 2 will end in 2020, meaning that security issues will not be resolved and additional improvements won't be made. Once Python 2 is officially retired, only Python 3.5 and later will see continued support. It is important to keep in mind that Python 2's syntax is a little different from Python 3's syntax. Due to Python 2's impending retirement, this book will not be teaching Python 2 and will only focus on Python 3.

1.4 - Installing Python

To ensure that you have Python installed correctly, go to the official Python website (https://www.python.org/downloads/), and follow the installation instructions. Currently, the Python website offers a simple executable to install Python on Windows and Mac OS.

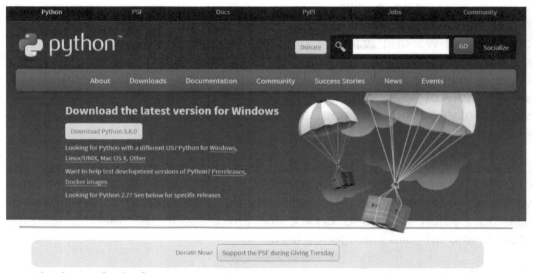

Looking for a specific release?

As the Windows version is the most easily accessible version of Python and since Windows is the most common OS, this book assumes that the reader is following along on a Windows OS. That said, if you are following along on a different OS, you don't need to worry. Differences between Python across systems are very minimal, usually restricted to differences in platform-specific libraries.

1.5 - Definitions: Interpreter, Terminal, Shell, IDE

Early on in this book, and as you continue to program in Python, you will see many references to concepts like "interpreter," "terminal," "shell," and "IDE." These concepts can be somewhat confusing for a beginner, so to make things simpler, let's define these concepts here. If you are already somewhat familiar with these programming concepts and just looking to learn Python as another language, feel free to skip this section.

```
Command Prompt - python                                                    —    □    ×
Python 3.6.6 (v3.6.6:4cf1f54eb7, Jun 27 2018, 03:37:03) [MSC v.1900 64 bit (AMD64)] on win32
Type "help", "copyright", "credits" or "license" for more information.
>>> _
```

An "interpreter" in the computer science/programming sense is a computer program that can execute code, carrying out the written instructions specified by a programming or scripting language. An interpreter carries out code immediately and directly. In contrast, a "compiler" is a program that translates instructions into efficient machine code. Meanwhile, a "shell" is a wrapper or environment whose primary function is to run other programs, and the word "shell" is often used to refer to the command-line of the OS. The command line takes in commands centered around the name of applications the user wishes to interact with. The interface you see above is an example of the Python shell that is running an interpreter.

Python has its own shell, an interactive interpreter specialized for running Python commands. It lets the user immediately execute Python code and see the result as soon as the user enters the command. The Python shell that can be accessed through the command-line is an example of a "terminal," which is simply the environment that allows the user to input text and receive outputs. For the purpose of this book, the terms "shell" and "terminal" may be used interchangeably in reference to an instance of the Python interpreter accessed through the command line.

1.6 - The Python Interpreter

There are two main ways to work with Python: with the interpreter and command line or with an Integrated Development Environment (IDE).

We will be doing most of our programming in an IDE, but first, let's make sure you understand how to work with Python in the terminal.

Let's start by opening the terminal/command prompt and checking that Python is installed correctly by just typing the command "python." If Python is properly installed, the command prompt should transition you to an instance of the Python interpreter/shell. This interpreter allows you to write and run Python code. For instance, if you copied this line of code into the terminal, you'd get "Using the terminal interpreter!" printed back out:

```
print ("Using the terminal interpreter!")
```

The command `print()` is responsible for printing out to the terminal whatever is specified inside the parentheses.

Most programming is done in an IDE, but it is still a good idea to learn how the Python interpreter works because there may be occasions where you may have to do some programming in it. With that in mind, let's take a few moments to familiarize ourselves with the Python interpreter.

As mentioned, the Python interpreter can typically be invoked from the command line simply by entering the command "Python," or perhaps the specific Python version you want to run:

```
python3.8
```

The interpreter can typically be exited with the quit command: `exit()` or depending on the version you are running `quit()`.

The `help()` command is incredibly helpful and you will always want to remember it because it will show you all the various commands and functions that you can use in the interpreter.

When you enter a command by hitting the enter/return key, the statement will be evaluated for correct syntax. If there is a syntax error, the error will be displayed.

Python is waiting for a command if you see the "primary prompt," which is often indicated by the presence of three greater-than signs (>>>). If you are on the second line of an input, these greater-than signs will instead be replaced with three periods (...).

1.7 - Using an IDE

I wanted to make you aware of the Python interpreter and the terminal's existence, but most of our programming will be done in an IDE. If you experiment with the terminal a little bit, you'll quickly find a major disadvantage of using the terminal. It's that you can't preserve many lines of code on the same screen. In addition, whenever you enter a line of code that contains errors, a syntax error will be thrown immediately. IDEs make the process of learning a language simpler because they will often highlight syntax errors for you. Other benefits of using an IDE include auto-completion for certain key phrases and functions, easier collaboration with other programmers, and the ability to make changes to a script even while an instance of the programming is running.

You can try out the code examples found in this book in either the terminal or in an IDE. However, most of the examples presented in this book will be presented in an IDE. One excellent IDE is PyCharm (https://www.jetbrains.com/pycharm), an open-source IDE designed from the ground up for use with Python. PyCharm highlights syntax errors, enables easy refactoring and renaming of files, and comes with an integrated debugger. PyCharm also has an integrated terminal, and when you run programs in PyCharm, the results of the program's execution will be displayed in the terminal at the bottom of the IDE.

PyCharm has a free version and a paid (Pro) version. Everything that this book covers can be done with the free version of the IDE. You don't need to pay for any features.

1.8 - Using PyCharm

Let's go over some of the functions in PyCharm in greater detail, so you're familiar with how to use them.

After installing PyCharm and setting it up for the first time, you may be slightly intimidated by all the options, but don't worry, you won't be using most of these options for the exercises in this book.

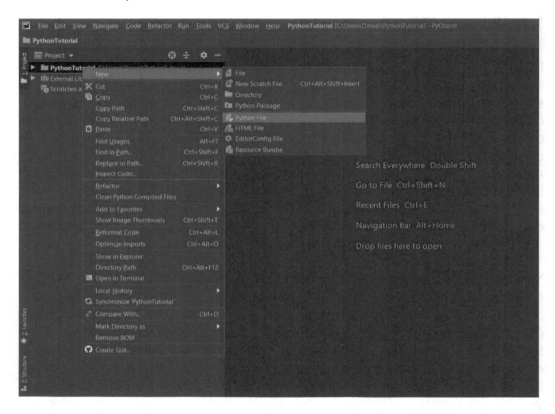

As you can see in the image above, when you open PyCharm and see the interface, you can navigate up to the file option in the top left corner. Opening the file drop-down menu will let you either open an existing project or create a new project. Opening an existing project enables you to reopen projects you've already started, saved, or even open projects that other people have worked on, which you have downloaded/cloned. For now, just create a new project for the exercises through the "File" option in the top left.

The New Project dialog box may look slightly different depending on which version of PyCharm you are using, but it should ask you to select a project interpreter. The default virtual environment (virtualenv) is fine for now, and it should automatically detect your base Python interpreter if it is correctly installed on your computer.

After this, you can create a folder to hold the scripts you create by right-clicking in the project frame and choosing the "New" option from the drop-down menu. To create a new Python script, just right-click on the folder you've created, navigate to "New," and then click the "Python File" option. Enter the name of your new file Python file.

After you create a new Python file, it should automatically open in the editor panel to the right. You can enter code into the editor. If, for some reason, the editor didn't automatically open the file, double-click on the file to open it up in the editor.

PyCharm should automatically save changes to the file, which means you don't need to worry about manually saving them. If, for some reason, the file doesn't auto-save, or you just want to be sure it has saved, you can right-click on the file to be presented with a drop-down menu that should contain the option to save the file. You can also press "Ctrl + S" to save all files currently open in PyCharm.

Once you've written some code and want to try running it, you can either navigate up to the "Run" tab on the top toolbar and select "Run (Current file name here)," or press "Shift + F10". The image below shows a program has finished its run in PyCharm's compiler. Note that the results of the program are printed to the built-in terminal at the bottom of the IDE.

Much like a regular text editing program, PyCharm provides you with some functions you can use to edit and control your code. For example, you can find specific bits of code by using the "Find" option. To open the find option, just type "Ctrl + F." You can also search the entire project for a block of code that matches a search term by using "Ctrl + Shift + F."

PyCharm is also equipped with a built-in debugger. The debugger can be activated the same way the file can be run: by right-clicking the file and selecting the "Debug" command. You can also press "Shift + F9." When you use the debugger, PyCharm will flag parts of your program where problems have been spotted. PyCharm also allows you to set breakpoints, which are points at which your program will be paused, which allows you to see how the data in your program has been manipulated up to that point.

PyCharm has more helpful features as well, like code completion and the automatic flagging of potential errors and formatting problems. PyCharm's code completion feature is a predictive-text feature that will analyze your code as you type and create a drop-down menu with possible options that you could use to complete your code. Meanwhile, PyCharm's code monitor will alert you to possible formatting and syntax errors. Notice how in the image below, syntax errors are underlined in red. It will also notify you of the Python style guide (PEP8) violations.

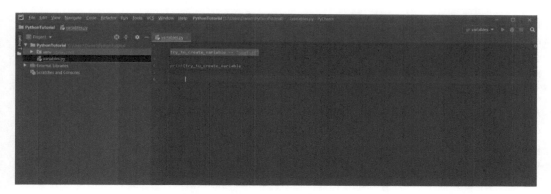

If you prefer not to use PyCharm and would like to use another IDE instead, that's okay. Some other excellent IDE's for Python include Spyder, PyDev, Idle, and Wing. Whatever IDE you choose to use, be sure that you devote some time to get familiar with what you can do with it. Good programmers work hard to understand every part of their toolkit.

1.9 - Good Programming Practices

As you follow along with this book and learn more about programming, it's highly advised that you learn the Python Style Guide and follow it as you write your code. PEP8 (https://www.python.org/dev/peps/pep-0008/), the Python style guide, lays out best practices for writing your code. These suggestions cover topics like when to use tabs or spaces, how to format import statements, suggested naming conventions for variables and classes, and much more.

Why is it a good idea to follow these style guides? There are two reasons: to help others and to help yourself.

Following Python standards helps others to read your code, as it should follow a template that others will have seen many times before. The PEP8 style guide is also structured to avoid ambiguous or confusing syntax, and the clarity of your code will assist other programmers in interpreting its purpose and functions. You don't want your code to be confusing to other programmers, as they will often be less willing to help you if your code is messy or hard to read.

Following the PEP8 standards will also aid you in understanding your code. It can be surprisingly easy to come back to a program that you have written a long time ago and forget what it does precisely, especially when the code is confusingly formatted.

As previously mentioned, PyCharm will notify you when you have broken certain PEP8 guidelines. While your code will probably still run if the only problems are style errors, you should still examine the PEP8 suggestions that PyCharm gives you and try to avoid making those errors in the future.

1.10 - Writing Comments in Python

As you write code in PyCharm, you'll notice that the code is in different colors. We'll cover what the colors mean exactly in later chapters, but for now, try replicating the code and running it:

```
# This is an example of a comment
# The code below prints out a statement
print ("Writing in an IDE!")
```

Notice that only "Writing in an IDE!" was returned and that the two lines which begin with "#" are ignored completely. Notice also that these two lines of code are represented in dark grey.

In Python, starting a line of code with the hash symbol/number sign (#) means that anything which follows the hash on that line is a "comment." The Python interpreter ignores comments because they aren't part of the commands that make up our program.

The purpose of comments is to leave notes for yourself and other developers—notes which aid in understanding the purpose of a chunk of code. It is highly advised that you add comments as you follow along with this book. Explaining what a chunk of code does will help you learn and better understand what commands accomplish what. Commenting on your code is also a good habit to get into, as it will help other developers understand the intention of your code.

One last note on comments: you can create a multi-line comment by using triple single quotes to open and close the comment block, like this:

```
'''
Comment line 1
Comment line 2
Comment line 3
'''
```

Chapter 2:
Variables and Operators

Now that we've gotten Python installed and an IDE set up, we're ready to begin learning Python for real. The following couple of chapters will focus on introducing core Python concepts like variables, operators, and the various types of data you can manipulate with Python. For now, let's concentrate on understanding variables and operators.

2.1 - Variables

When you hear the word "variable," what do you think of? There's a good chance you might think back to algebra class and recall that a variable was often a letter that represents some number. In other words, it was an item that contained a representation of another item. Generally, in Python and programming, that's what variables are. They are just representations of data stored in a form that is easy to access and manipulate. Let's try creating some variables now.

```
X = 30
```

That's a very common usage of a variable. Just like you'd see in math class, "X" represents the numerical value 30. However, variables can also store other types of data, like text.

```
weather = "cloudy"
```

Here, we're asserting that the "weather" variable has the word "cloudy" stored in it. When we use the "equals" sign in Python, unlike in math, we aren't saying that the two values are equal. Rather, we're "assigning" or storing a value in that variable. We'll talk more about this when we cover operators, but for now, just know that in Python (and in programming languages generally), the equals sign is used differently than the mathematical equals sign.

As far as naming our variables goes, a variable can basically be called anything if the name adheres to a few rules:

- It contains only letters, numbers, or underscores
- The first character is not a number
- The variable name is not one of the reserved keywords

Uppercase and lowercase letters are fine, as are any amount of numbers or underscores, although the first character in the variable name cannot be a number. There are also a few words (like "input," "print," and "while") that cannot be used as variable names because Python reserves these words for specific commands. One last important thing to remember is that variable names are case sensitive, so "varName" is a different variable than "varname."

While variables can be named pretty much anything, in practice, you'll want to follow some guidelines when creating variable names. In the past, there were two commonly accepted ways of formatting variable names: camel case and snake case. Camel case refers to the practice of joining together compound words with upper case letters (i.e. variableName, thisIsCamelCase). Meanwhile, snake case is just adding underscores between compound variable names, like this: underscore_name, variable_name, this_is_snake_case.

According to the Python style guide, the preferred variable style is snake case.

Beyond that, try to name variables things that make sense. Avoid confusing variable names (i.e. Cat = "dog") in favor of variable names that make intuitive sense (animal = "dog").

2.2 - Operators

Now that we've discussed variables, let's talk about operators. Operators are symbols that perform functions, and they are used to manipulate data in different ways.

We've already touched on one operator, the assignment operator, which is represented by an equal sign. As previously mentioned, the "=" sign in Python has a different meaning than its use in math; here it means that we are assigning the value on the right side of the operator to the variable name found on the left side. Let's try using the = operator and assigning some values to some variables.

```
R = 12
S = 9
T = S
```

Let's now print out the values of these variables.

```
print(R)
print(S)
print(T)
```

Notice that the output of the program is 12, 9, 9. This is because we assigned the value 12 to the variable R, the value 9 to the variable S, and then assigned the variable S to the variable T, meaning T will contain the same value as S.

Now let's look at some of the other operators found in Python. The operators that are found in Python include the addition operator, the subtraction operator, the multiplication operator, the division operator, the floor division operator, the modulus operator, and the exponent operator.

The addition operator: +
The addition operator adds two values together.
Example: If R = 2 and S = 3, then R + S = 5

The subtraction operator: -
The subtraction operator subtracts the second value from the first.
Example: If R = 4 and S = 3, then R - S = 1

The multiplication operator: *
The multiplication operator multiplies two values.
Example: If R = 3 and S = 2, then R * S = 6

The division operator: /

The division operator divides the second value into the first.
Example: If R = 9 and S = 3, then R / S = 3
The floor division operator: //
The floor division operator divides and then rounds down to the nearest whole number.
Example: If R = 7 and S = 2, then R // S = 3

The Modulus Operator: %
The Modulus operator produces the remainder of a division operation.
Example: If R = 7 and S = 2, then R % S = 1

The Exponent Operator: **
The Exponent operator raises the first value to the power of the second value.
Example: If R = 9 and S = 2, R**S = 81

It's highly advised that you play around with these operators and try writing programs that use them in order to get familiar with their different use cases.

2.3 - Combining Operators

The assignment operator can be combined with other operators like addition, subtraction, and multiplication operators. This makes it easier to carry out operations in one step instead of multiple steps. To be clearer, here's an example:

Instead of having to write:

```
R = R * 2
```

We could just write:

```
R *= 2
```

Try experimenting with the other combined operators to see how easy they make updating values.

Chapter 3:
Data Types

3.1 - Data Types

Now that we've discussed the basic operators that can be used in Python, we can move on to a discussion about data types. Computer programming languages have several different methods of storing and interacting with data, and these different methods of representation are the data types you'll interact with. The primary data types within Python are integers, floats, and strings. These data types are stored in Python using different data structures, such as lists, tuples, and dictionaries. We'll get into data structures after we address the topic of data types.

Integers in Python aren't different from what you were taught in math class: a whole number or a number that possess no decimal points or fractions. Numbers like 4, 9, 39, -5, and 1215 are all integers. Integers can be stored in variables just by using the assignment operator, as we have seen in Chapter 2.

Floats are numbers that possess decimal parts. This makes numbers like -2.049, 12.78, 15.1, 8.0, and 0.23 floats. The method of creating a float instance in Python is the same as declaring an integer: just choose a name for the variable and then use the assignment operator.

While we've mainly dealt with numbers so far, Python can also interpret and manipulate text data. Text data is referred to as a "string," and you can think of it as the letters that are strung together in a word or series of words. To create an instance of a string in Python, you can use either double quotes or single quotes as shown below.

```
string_1 = "This is a string."
string_2 = 'This is also a string.'
```

However, while either double or single quotes can be used, it is recommended that you use double quotes when possible. This is because there may be times you need to nest quotes within quotes. Using the traditional format of single quotes within double quotes is the encouraged standard.

Something to keep in mind when using strings is that numerical characters surrounded by quotes are treated as a string and not as a number.

```python
# The 97 here is a string

stringy = "97"

# Here it is a number

numerical = 97
```

3.2 - String Manipulation

When it comes to manipulating strings, we can combine strings the exact way we combine numbers. All you must do is insert an addition operator in between two strings to combine them. Try replicating the code below:

```python
str_1 = "Words "
str_2 = "and "
str_3 = "more words."

str_4 = str_1 + str_2 + str_3

print(str_4)
```

What you should get back is: "Words and more words."

Python provides several easy-to-use, built-in commands to alter strings. For instance, adding .upper() to a string will make all characters in the string uppercase, while using .lower() on the string will make all the characters in the string lowercase. These commands are called "functions," and we'll discuss them in greater detail later in the book. For now, know that Python has already done much of the heavy lifting for you when it comes to manipulating strings.

```
uppercase_string = "all uppercase".upper()
print(uppercase_string)
```

What you should get back is: "ALL UPPERCASE"

3.3 - String Formatting

Another method of manipulating strings include string formatting, accomplished with the "%" operator. We discussed the fact that the "%" symbol returns remainders when carrying out mathematical operations, but it has another use when working with strings. In the context of strings, the % symbol allows you to specify values/variables you would like to insert into a string and then have the string filled in with those values in specified areas. You can think of it like sorting a bunch of labeled items (the values beyond the % symbol) into bins (the holes in the string you've marked with %).

Try running this bit of code to see what happens:

```
string_to_print = "With the modulus operator, you can
add %s, integers like %d, or even floats like %2.1f."
% ("strings", 25, 12.34)

print (string_to_print)
```

The output of the print statement should be as follows:

"With the modulus operator, you can add strings, integers like 25, or even floats like 12.3."

The "s" modifier after the % is used to denote the placement of strings, while the "d" modifier is used to indicate the placement of integers. Finally, the "f" modifier is used to indicate the placement of floats, and the decimal notation between the "%" and "f" is used to declare how many digits need to be displayed. For instance, if the modulator is used like this %2.1, it means you need two digits before the decimal place and one digit after the decimal place displayed, hence 12.3 was printed out even though we gave 12.34.

There's another way to format strings in Python. You can use the built-in "format" function. We'll go into what functions are exactly in later chapters, but for now, we just need to understand that Python provides us with a handy shortcut to avoid having to type out the modulus operator whenever we want to format a string. Instead, we can just write something like the following:

"The string you want to format {} ".format(values you want to insert).

The braces denote the location where you want to insert the value. To insert multiple values, all you need to do is create multiple braces and then separate the values with commas. In other words, you would type something like this:

```
string_to_print = "With the modulus operator, you can
add {0:s}, integers like {1:d}, or even floats like
{2:2.2f}."

print(string_to_print.format("strings", 25, 12.34))
```

Inside the brackets goes the data type tag and the position of the value in the collection of values you want to place in that spot. Try shifting the numbers in the brackets above around and see how they change. Remember that Python, unlike some other programming languages, is a zero-based system when it comes to positions, meaning that the first item in a list of items is always said to be at position zero/0 and not one/1.

One last thing to mention about string formatting in Python is that if you are using the format function and don't care to manually indicate where a value should go, you can simply leave the brackets blank. Doing so will have Python automatically fill in the brackets, in order from left to right, with the values in your list ordered from left to right (the first bracket gets the first item in the list, the second bracket gets the second item, etc.).

3.4 - Type Casting

The term "type casting" refers to the act of converting data from one type to another type. As you program, you may often find out that you need to convert data between types. There are three helpful commands in Python that will allow the quick and easy conversion between data types: `int()`, `float()` and `str()`.

All three of the above commands convert what is placed within the parenthesis to the data type outside the parentheses. This means that to convert a float into an integer, you would write the following:

```
int(float here)
```

Because integers are whole numbers, anything after the decimal point in a float is dropped when it is converted into an integer (i.e. 3.9324 becomes 3, 4.12 becomes 4). Note that you cannot convert a non-numerical string into an integer, so typing: int("convert this") would throw an error.

The `float()` command can convert integers or certain strings into floats. Providing either an integer or an integer in quotes (a string representation of an integer) will convert the provided value into a float. Both 5 and "5" become 5.0.

Finally, the `str()` function is responsible for the conversion of integers and floats to strings. Plug in any numerical value into the parenthesis and get back a string representation of it.

We've covered a fair amount of material so far. Before we go any further, let's do an exercise to make sure you understand the material we've covered thus far.

3.5 - Assignment and Formatting Exercise

Here's an assignment. Write a program that does the following:

- Assigns a numerical value to a variable and changes the value in some way
- Assigns a string value to some variable
- Prints the string and then the value by using string formatting
- Converts the numerical data into a different format and prints the new data form

Give it your best shot before looking below for an example of how this can be done.

Ready to see an example of how this can be accomplished? See below:

```
R = 9
R = 9 / 3
stringy = "There will be a number following this
sentence: {}".format(R)
print(stringy)
R = str(R)
print(R)
```

Chapter 4:
Data Structures

We've already covered data types. Now we will shift to discuss the other important part of handling data - how the data is stored. The way data is stored is called its structure, and there are many different data structures in Python. The primary data structures in Python are Lists, Tuples, and Dictionaries.

4.1 - Lists

Lists are collections of data. When you think about a list in regular life, you often think of a grocery list or a to-do list. These lists are collections of items, and that's precisely what lists in Python are: collections of items. Lists are convenient because they offer quick and easy storage and retrieval of items.

Let's say we have several values that we need to access in our program. We could declare separate variables for all those values, or we could store them all in a single variable as a list. Declaring a list is as simple as using brackets and separating objects in the list with commas. So, if we wanted to declare a list of fruits, we could do that by doing the following:

```
Fruits = ["apple", "pear", "orange", "banana"]
```

It's also possible to declare an empty list by just using empty brackets. You can later add items to the list with a specific function, the append function - `append()`. We can access the items in the list individually by specifying the position of the item that we want. Remember, Python is zero-based, so the first item in the list has a position of 0. How do we utilize the values from a list? We just declare a variable that references that specific value and position, as shown below:

```
Apple = fruits[0]
```

If you want to start by selecting items from the end of the list first, instead of the front of the list, you can do this by using negative numbers. Passing "-1" into the brackets will give us the last item in the list while passing "-2" will select the second to last item. As you saw above, you can choose one item from a list and store it as a variable, but you can also choose multiple items from a list. This is achieved using the colon inside the brackets, with the value on the left of the colon indicating the first value you'd like to select and the value on the right side of the colon indicating where to stop selecting values. This means that if you had a list containing 6 items, the notation `list[1:4]` would select the second item in the list (remember, zero-based) through the fourth item.

This style of using brackets and colons to select portions of a list is known as list slicing. Remember that when slicing a list, the slicing notation takes the item you want to get first as the first input and the item you want to end your search at as the second input. In order words, the item at the first index is included, but the item at the second index isn't. Going back to our list of fruits, if we sliced that list like so [0:2], we would only get "apple" and "pear" included in the slice because the second input specifies where we stop searching, which is the third value on the list.

You can also slice with the assistance of a third input, referred to as a stepper. If you had a list of numbers running from 0 to 8, you could slice it by getting every other number instead of every number from a starting point to an endpoint. Let's assume we want to slice the list of numbers and get every other number. We could do this by using the following commands:

```
numbers = [0, 1, 2, 3, 4, 5, 6, 7, 8]
numbers[0:9:2]
```

This notation instructs the interpreter to start at 0 and run until 9, getting every second number. The return value is a list, as shown below:

```
[0, 2, 4, 6, 8]
```

When slicing, default values will be used if you don't specify an input. For instance, the default value for the first input is the beginning of the list, while on the opposite end, the default value for the second input is the end of the list. This means that a slice like [:12] would start from the first item and run until the eleventh item on the list. In other words, [:12] is a shorthand version of writing [0:12].

Lists can be modified in several different ways. Items can be added or removed from the list, but the value of individual items in the list can be altered as well. To change the value of an item in a list, you declare which index of the list you want to alter, followed by the value you want to replace it with. For example, you could update the fourth item on a list to a value of 15 by doing the following:

```
Numbers[3] = 15
```

Adding items to a list can be accomplished with the `append()` function. The value you want to append to the list just goes inside the parentheses. Call the function with a period and the function name after the list you want to append the item to. In other words:

```
list_to_update.append(value)
```

The append function adds a new item to the end of the list. With the remove function, you can delete an item from the list. You just need to specify the index of the item that you want to remove when using the function. You write `del` followed by the index of the item or items in the list you would like to remove. For instance, the following code would drop the values starting at index two and ending at index four from the list "A." Please note that the last index is not inclusive, meaning the item at index 4 will not be deleted in this example.

```
del A[2:4]
```

If you would like to remove a specific value, you could use the `remove()` function. The `remove()` function will remove the first item from the list that matches the input value. Please note that if your list contains multiple entries of that value, `remove()` function will only remove one entry, not all entries of that value.

```
list_to_update.remove(value)
```

If you want to insert values at a specific position in a list, you can use the `insert()` function. The `insert()` function takes in two values, the first of which is the index where you'd like to insert the value, and the second is the value that you want to insert. Insertions are made immediately before the specified index, so the specified index and everything after it will have their indexes bumped up by one.

The following command would have the effect of inserting a 12 before the fourth item in list "A."

```
A.insert(3, 12)
```

There's one more thing we should cover about lists. As you continue to learn about data structures and algorithms, you'll hear about lists and a related structure called an "array." When used outside of a Python programming context (i.e. in a general data structures context), an "array" is just a list of indexed items. In this pure data structure sense, a "list" is an improved version of an array that has more functionality, like the ability to be resized or the ability to have links between items that point to the next item in the list.

Python has arrays as well, in addition to lists. In Python, arrays allow you to access and manipulate the items directly. If you wanted to divide every element in an array by 4, you could do this easily. In contrast, trying to divide a list by 4 will throw an error. In practice, arrays don't see much use outside of mathematical and data science programming. If you intend to get into these fields, you should investigate arrays further, but for our purposes, we won't spend time delving into them as we did with lists.

4.2 - Tuples

Tuples are very similar to lists, but unlike lists, their contents cannot be modified once they are created. Items that exist in tuples when created will exist for as long as the tuple exists. If it's unclear as to when tuples would be useful, imagine if you have a list of items that will never change. For example, consider the days of the week. A list containing all the days of the week won't change. In practice, you are likely to use tuples far less often than you will use lists, but it's good to be aware of the existence of tuples.

Functionally, tuples are declared and accessed very similarly to lists. The major difference is that when a tuple is created, parentheses are used instead of brackets, as shown below:

```
This_is_a_tuple = ("these", "are", "values", "in",
"a", "tuple")
```

The items can be accessed with brackets, just like a list.

```
Word = this_is_a_tuple[0]
```

4.3 - Dictionaries

Dictionaries hold data that can be retrieved with reference items, or keys. Dictionaries can be confusing for first-time programmers, but imagine a bank filled with numerous safety deposit boxes. There are rows and rows of these boxes, and the contents of each box can only be accessed when the correct key is provided. Much like opening a deposit box, the correct key must be provided to retrieve the value within a dictionary. In other words, dictionaries contain pairs of keys and values that are associated with those keys.

When you declare a dictionary, you must provide both the value and the key that will be associated with that value. These keys must be unique. Evidently, it would be a problem if one key could open multiple boxes, so keys in a dictionary cannot be repeated; you cannot have two keys, both named "Key1."

The syntax for creating a key in Python is to use curly braces containing the key on the left side and the value on the right side, separated by a colon. To demonstrate, here is an example of a dictionary:

```
Dict_example = {"key1": 39}
```

39

If you want to create a dictionary with multiple items, all you need to do is separate the items with commas.

```
Dict_example2 = {"key1": 39, "key2": 21, "key3": 54}
```

Dictionaries can also be declared by using the `dict()` method. You could create the same dictionary as above with keys and their values by using the assignment operator and separating them with commas.

```
Dict_example3  = dict(key1 = 39, key2 = 21, key3 = 54)
```

Note that this method uses parentheses instead of curly braces and doesn't use quotes.

To access items within the dictionary, you need to supply the appropriate key. The syntax for this in Python is `dictionary['key']`, so in order to get 39 from the dictionary above, you can use the syntax below:

```
number = Dict_example3["key1"]
```

Since the syntax above will output the value associated with the provided key, you might be able to guess that we can overwrite the value of a given key by referencing that given key and using an assignment operator:

```
Dict_example3["key1"] = 99
```

Much like how it is possible to create an empty list with just an empty pair of square brackets, we can also create an empty dictionary by using empty curly braces when we declare the dictionary.

```
Dict_example4 = { }
```

To add data to a dictionary, all we need to do is create a new dictionary key and assign a value to it.

```
Dict_example4["key1"] = 109
```

To drop values from the dictionary, we use the `del` command followed by the dictionary and the key we want to drop.

```
del Dict_example4["key1"]
```

We're now going to move on to the next topic: interactivity, inputs, and handling outputs.

4.4 - Data Structures Exercise

Before we move on to the next topic, let's take a moment to make sure we understand the data structures we've covered. Try writing a program that does the following:

- Creates a list.
- Alters the content of the list.
- Extracts one item from the list and saves it as a variable.
- Stores the value in a dictionary with a key pointing to it.
- Adds more key-value pairs to the dictionary.
- Retrieves and prints the stored dictionary value by accessing it with a key.

Try to solve the problem yourself before looking below for a possible answer to the exercise prompt.

If you've tried writing your own program and are ready to proceed onward, your answer might have turned out to be something like this:

```
list_1 = ["keys", "wallet", "hat", "glasses", "phone"]

list_1.append("headphones")
list_1.remove("hat")

glasses = list_1[2]

dict_1 = dict(key1 = glasses, key2 = "coffee mug",
key3 = "cat food")

print(dict_1['key1'])
```

(A note on the exercises in this book: If your solution differed from the solution provided above, that's completely fine. There are several ways to solve programming problems, and the solution provided above isn't necessarily the best one. A huge part of your job as a programmer will be balancing the solutions that work for you, while creating elegant and simple solutions.)

Chapter 5:
Inputs, Printing, and Formatting Outputs

5.1 - Inputs

So far, we've only been writing programs that only use data we have explicitly defined in the script. However, your programs can also take in input from a user and utilize it. Python lets us solicit inputs from the user with a very intuitively named function - the `input()` function. Utilizing the `input()` function enables us to prompt the user to enter information, which we can further manipulate. For example, we can take the user's input and save it as a variable, print it straight to the terminal, or do anything else we might like.

When we use the input function, we can pass in a string. The user will see this string as a prompt, and their response to the prompt will be saved as the input value. For instance, if we wanted to query the user for their favorite food, we could write the following:

```
favorite_food = input("What is your favorite food?: ")
```

If you ran this code example, you would be prompted to input your favorite food. You could save multiple variables this way and print them all at once using the `print()` function along with print formatting, as we covered earlier. To be clear, the text that you write in the input function is what the user will see as a prompt; it isn't what you are inputting into the system as a value.

When you run the code above, you'll be prompted for an input. After you type in some text and hit the enter/return key, the text you wrote will be stored as the variable `favorite_food`. The input command can be used along with string formatting to inject variables into the text prompt that the user will see. For instance, if we had a variable called *user_name* that stored the name of the user, we could structure the input statement like this:

```
favorite_food = input("What is {}'s favorite
food?:".format("Your name here"))
```

5.2 - Printing and Formatting Outputs

We've already dealt with the `print()` function quite a bit, but let's take some time to address it again here and learn a bit more about its advanced features.

By now, you've gathered that it prints out whatever is in the parentheses of the function to the terminal. In addition, you've learned that you can format the printing of statements with either the modulus operator (%) or the format function (`.format()`). However, what should we do if we are in the process of printing a very long message?

In order to prevent a long string from running across the screen, we can use triple quotes to surround our string. Printing with triple quotes allows us to separate our print statements onto multiple lines. For example, we could print like this:

```
print('''By using triple quotes we can
divide our print statement onto multiple
lines, making it easier to read.''')
```

Formatting the print statement like that will give us:

By using triple quotes we can
divide our print statement onto multiple
lines, making it easier to read.

What if we need to print characters that are equivalent to string formatting instructions? For example, if we ever needed to print out the characters "%s" or "%d", we would run into trouble. If you recall, these are string formatting commands, and if we try to print these out, the interpreter will interpret them as formatting commands.

Here's a practical example. As mentioned, typing "/t" in our string will put a tab in the middle of our string. Assume we type the following:

```
print("We want a \t here, not a tab.")
```

We'd get back this:

We want a   here, not a tab.

By using an escape character, we can tell Python to include the characters that come next as part of the string's value. The escape character we want to use is the "raw string" character, an "r" before the first quote in a string, like this:

```
print(r"We want a \t here, not a tab.")
```

So, if we used the raw string, we'd get the format we want back:

We want a \t here, not a tab.

The "raw string" formatter enables you to put any combination of characters you'd like within the string and have it be considered as part of the string's value.

However, what if we did want the tab in the middle of our string? In that case, using special formatting characters in our string is referred to as using "escape characters." "Escaping" a string is a method of reducing the ambiguity in how characters are interpreted. When we use an escape character, we escape the typical method that Python uses to interpret certain characters, and the characters we type are understood to be part of the string's value. The escape primarily used in Python is the backslash (\). The backslash prompts Python to listen for a unique character to follow that will be translated to a specific string formatting command.

We already saw that using the "\t" escape character puts a tab in the middle of our string, but there are other escape characters we can use as well and they are shown below:

\n - Starts a new line

45

\\- Prints out a backslash itself

\" - Prints out a double quote instead of a double quote marking the end of a string

\' - Like above, but prints out a single quote

5.3 - Input and Formatting Exercise

Let's do another exercise that applies what we've covered in this section. You should try to write a program that does the following:

- Prompts the user for answers to several different questions
- Prints out the answers on different lines using a single print statement

Give this a shot before you look below for a solution to this exercise prompt.

If you've given this a shot, your answer might look something like this:

```
favorite_food = input("What's your favorite food? :")
favorite_animal = input("What about your favorite animal? :")
favorite_movie = input("What's the best movie? :")

print("Favorite food is: " + favorite_food + "\n" +
      "Favorite animal is: " + favorite_animal + "\n"
+
      "Favorite movies is: " + favorite_movie)
```

We've covered a lot of ground in the first quarter of this book. In the next section, we'll begin covering some more complex topics and concepts. However, before we move on, let's be sure that we've got the basics down. It won't be easy learning the new concepts unless you are familiar with what we've already covered so far, so for that reason, let's do a quick review of what we've learned:

Chapters 1 - 5 Review

Variables - Variables are representations of values. They contain the value and allow the value to be manipulated without having to write it out every time. Variable names must contain only letters, numbers, or underscores. In addition, the first character in a variable name cannot be a number, and the variable name must not be one of Python's reserved keywords.

Operators - Operators are symbols which are used to manipulate data. The assignment operator (=) is used to store values in variables. Other operators in Python include the addition operator (+), the subtraction operator (–), the multiplication operator (*), the division operator(/), the floor division operator (//), the modulus operator (%), and the exponent operator (**). The mathematical operators can be combined with the assignment operator (i.e. +=, –=, *=).

Strings - Strings are text data, declared by wrapping text in single or double-quotes. There are two methods of formatting strings; with the modulus operator or the .format() command. The "s," "d," and "f" modifiers are used to specify the placement of strings, integers, and floats.

Integers - Integers are whole numbers, numbers that possess no decimal points or fractions. Integers can be stored in variables simply by using the assignment operator.

Floats - Floats are numbers that possess decimal parts. The method of creating a float in Python is the same as declaring an integer, just choose a name for the variable and then use the assignment operator.

Type Casting - Type casting allows you to convert one data type to another if the conversion is feasible (non-numerical strings cannot be converted into integers or floats). You can use the following functions to convert data types: int(), float() and str().

Lists - Lists are just collections of data, and they can be declared with brackets and commas separating the values within the brackets. Empty lists can also be created. List items can be accessed by specifying the position of the desired item. The `append()` function is used to add an item to a list, while the `del` command and `remove()` functions can be used to remove items from a list.

List Slicing - List slicing is a method of selecting values from a list. The item at the first index is included, but the item at the second index isn't. A third value, a stepper value, can also be used to slice the list, skipping through the array at a rate specified by the value (i.e. - numbers[0:9:2]). If a stepper value is not provided then it will be defaulted to 1, meaning it will increment through the indexes 1 at a time.

Tuples - Tuples are like lists, but they are immutable; unlike lists, their contents cannot be modified once they are created. When a tuple is created, parentheses are used instead of brackets.

Dictionaries - Dictionaries store data in key-value pairs. When a dictionary is declared, the value and the key that will be used to reference that value must be specified. In addition, key-value pairs must be unique. The syntax for creating a dictionary in Python is curly braces containing the key on the left side and the value on the right side, separated by a colon (i.e. - my_dictionary = {"my_key": "my_value"}).

Inputs - The `input()` function gets an input from the user. A string is passed into the parenthesis, which the user will see when they are prompted to enter a string or numerical value.

Print Formatting - Triple quotes allow us to separate print statements onto multiple lines. Escape characters are used to denote that special formatting characters, like "\n" and "\t," should be included in a string's value. Meanwhile, the "raw string" command, "r," can be used to include all the characters within the quotes.

Chapter 6:
Conditional Statements and Control Flow Statements

Now that we've covered the basics of Python syntax, we can move on to more complex topics. In the following chapters, you'll learn how to handle conditions, how to create and use functions, as well as learn about the concepts of object-oriented programming and classes. We'll start with a look at conditions and conditional logic.

6.1 - Handling Conditions

We'll go over conditions and conditional logic in this section. As you write your own programs, you'll need to carry out specific actions based on certain conditions. Conditional statements are used to evaluate whether these certain conditions are being met. If the conditions are being met, one set of actions will be carried out, and if the conditions aren't being met, another set of actions will be carried out. While the conditional statements are used to evaluate a condition, control flow statements are used to control the execution of what occurs after a condition has been evaluated.

Let's look at conditional statements and how they are used.

6.2 - Conditional Statements

The comparison statement is the most commonly used conditional statement. The comparison statement is a double equals sign (==), and it checks to see if two values are equivalent to each other. As an example, if B = 9 and C = 9, the statement B == C will be evaluated as True.

Meanwhile, if `B = 12` and `C = 4`, and the same comparison statement is written, the statement is evaluated as `False`.

There are other comparison operators that you can use, and they are probably similar to those you learned in math class.

The "smaller/less than" operator (<) checks that the value on the left is smaller than the value on the right. The "greater/larger than" operator (>) checks to see that the value on the left is greater than the value on the right. There are also the "less than or equal to" (<=) and the "greater than or equal to" (>=) operators. These operators function like the less than and greater than operators, but they will also evaluate whether the two values are equal. If so, the statement be evaluated as `True`.

Another operator is the "not equals" operator (!=). The not equals operator checks to see if two values are unequal; it will evaluate as `True` if the two values are different, and `False` if the two values are equal. The order of the values does not matter, unlike with the less than/greater than operators, since the not equals operator is only checking to see if two values are non-equivalent.

Here are some examples of how the operators can be used:

Greater Than: 9 > 3

Greater Than or Equal to: 12 >= 12

Less Than: 2 < 9

Less Than or Equal to: 4 <= 4

Not Equals: 9 != 15

These comparison operators can also be combined with three different logical operators. Logical operators are used to tell the computer that it must take multiple conditions into account, not just one. For example, you could check to make sure that a value falls in a middle range by requiring the value is both less than some number and greater than some other number. The three logical operators are *and*, *or*, *not*.

The and operator is used to state that all the provided conditions must be true for the overall statement to be evaluated as True. If one portion of the statement is False, the whole statement will be evaluated as False. For example, if a statement like 7 < 2 and 3 == 3 will be evaluated as False.

The or operator is used to check if one part of a statement is true. If at least one part of a statement is true, then the entire statement is evaluated as True. For a statement with an or operator included in it to be evaluated as False, all parts of the statement must be false. For example, the following statement is True, because just one part of the statement needs to be true: 5 == 5 or 9 > 12.

The not operator is used to check that the next condition is False. This is a double negative, and the not operator will return True if the provided condition isn't true. This can be confusing at first, but play around with the not operator, and you'll come to understand it. As an example, the statement not 12 > 15, will evaluate as True since 12 is not greater than 15.

6.3 - Control Flow Statements

We've covered how conditional statements are used to check if certain conditions are True or False, so now we can cover control flow statements. Control flow statements are used to control *how* data will be manipulated according to the conditional statements provided. Typically, statements inside a program are executed in order of their appearance, from top to bottom. Control flow statements alter the order in which statements are executed.

There are three commonly used control flow statements: `if`, `for`, `while`. In addition to these control flow statements, two different statements can also be used to handle errors that may occur when using control flow statements. Let's look at the three control flow statements first.

6.4 - If Statement

The `if` statement is used to allow programs to check whether a certain condition has been fulfilled. If the provided condition is met, then the program will carry out the specified action that follows. The `if` statement is telling the computer to "do this only if this condition is met." The `if` statement is used in conjunction with another control flow operator: the `else` statement. The `else` command is used to specify what the computer should do if the provided criteria isn't met. Therefore, an `else` statement must come after an `if` statement.

Here's an example of the structure of `if`/`else` control flow:

```
if R is True:
    Do S
else:
    Do T
```

Notice that the sections which define what action should be taken are indented. The colon/indent combo is how Python handles conditional logic and control flow statements. This is one of the ways Python syntax differs from other languages like Java or C, which often use parentheses or brackets to specify what actions should be carried out when a condition is met.

It's possible to use multiple `if/else` conditional checks in one code block. By doing this, you can handle multiple conditions that might occur. In order to accomplish this, you can use the `elif` statement, which stands for "else if." You just add the `elif` statement below the original `if` statement. It is also possible for you to add as many `elif` statements as you wish. The final statement that exits the conditional checks should be the `else` statement. Below is an example of how you could use the `elif` statement in a program:

```
if A is True:
     Do B
elif C is True:
     Do D
elif E is True:
     Do F
else:
     Do Z
```

It's also possible to write `if` and `else` statements inline, meaning that the logic is specified in the same line that executes as the command, like assigning a variable or printing something. Writing the statements inline means you don't have to break up the control flow statements onto different lines by using colons and indents. Here's an example of how this can be done:

```
outdoors = "Possible" if weather == "sunny" else "not
possible"
```

The above code would set the variable, `outdoors`, to a value of `Possible` if the value of the variable `weather` equals `sunny`. If not, then `outdoors` is set to `not possible`. While writing control flow statements, inline is possible and convenient when doing a simple check on a value. However, it's less clear than the regular way of formatting, and it can be confusing to new programmers. For that reason, this book will use the regular control flow formatting method when handling conditional logic.

Let's review an example that will run in PyCharm so you can see how this all comes together. Suppose you are creating a game and want to ask the player to choose a difficulty level as shown below:

```
difficulty = input("Choose '1' for 'Easy', '2' for
'Normal', '3' for 'Hard', or '4' for 'Impossible': ")

if difficulty == "1":
    print("Easy difficulty chosen.")
elif difficulty == "2":
    print("Normal difficulty chosen.")
elif difficulty == "3":
    print("Hard difficulty chosen.")
elif difficulty == "4":
    print("Impossible difficulty chosen.")
else:
    print("Please enter a valid difficulty.")
```

The above program prompts the user to enter a level of difficulty and prints back their chosen difficulty. If a value that isn't one of the four difficulties is inputted, it will tell the user to `"Please enter a valid difficulty."`

6.5 - For Loops and While

Let's look at the next type of control flow statement, the `for` statement. `for` statements are used to start off "for loops." A "for loop" is used to tell the computer that you want to keep executing a block of code until a specified condition has been met or until it is otherwise no longer valid. `for` loops are used to iterate through a series of items, meaning to proceed through the series one by one. If you have a list of items, you can iterate through that list. You can also iterate through tuples and dictionaries. Any series of items you can iterate through is referred to as an "iterable." The syntax for looping through iterables is shown below:

```
iterable = [1, 2, 3]

for x in iterable:
    print(x)
```

If we assumed that the iterable above is a list containing ten items, then the command above would iterate through and print out each item one by one until reaching the end of the list. To be clearer, here's an example you can run in PyCharm:

```
cats = ['Kitana', 'Fluffy', 'Ben', 'Cookie']

for cat in cats:
    print(cat + " has been fed.")
```

If you run the code above, you will get the name of the cat followed by "has been fed." The program will run through and assign the first cat to the stored value and run the print statement below it. It will then do the same for the second cat, and so on.

In the code above, we used `cat` as the name of the variable in the `for` loop. However, this could have been called `x` or `i` or pretty much anything we wanted. Python interprets the variable name we provide in that spot as the variable that references the list entry in the loop being executed. Try changing the `cat` variable above and notice that the code still executes no matter what you call the variable. Please note that you will need to change the variable name both in the `for` statement and in the print function to match each other.

In addition to dealing with the values in the list, we can get the index of those values. This can be accomplished by using the function `enumerate()`. To retrieve the index of a value with the `enumerate()` function in a `for` loop, you can declare two variables – one for the value of the item and one for the index of the item. For example:

```
Items_list = [10, 9, 8, 7, 6, 5]
for index, item in enumerate(items_list):
    print(index, item)
```

You can loop through a dictionary in much the same way that you can loop through a list or tuple. However, the variable you provide will only capture the key and not the value. If you want to get access to both the key and value in the dictionary, you need to specify that you want to access the dictionary elements after the colon in the `for` loop:

```
drinks = {'drink_1': 'coffee', 'drink_2': 'tea'}

for i in drinks:
    print ("Drink number = {}, drink = {}".format(i,
drinks[i]))
```

There's another way to do this as well, you can use the `items()` function, which will return the key and data as a tuple. You can then access the individual elements of that tuple.

```
drinks = {'drink_1':'coffee', 'drink_2':'tea'}

for i, j in drinks.items():
```

```
    print ("Drink number = {}, drink = {}".format(i,
j))
```

Much like you can loop through lists, tuples, and dictionaries, you can also loop through strings. The syntax is the same as looping through a list, just declare the variable and loop through it.

```
stringy = 'A string.'
for i in stringy:
    print(i)
```

Looping through a series of numbers can be done easily by making use of the `range()` function. The `range()` function will create an iterable list based on your chosen input parameters. The syntax for using the range function is as follows:

```
range(start, end, step)
```

If you haven't specified a start value, the list will start from zero by default. The ending parameter specifies where the function should stop generating numbers, but the value itself won't be included in the generated list of numbers. If a step value hasn't been provided, by default, the step value will be one, and the numbers will be generated consecutively.

The code below is expected to print out the numbers 0 to 10, with a number on every line:

```
for x in range(11):
    print(x)
```

Now that we've covered the `if` and `for` control flow statements, we're going to examine the `while` loop. The `while` loop is used to carry out a command or group of commands, while a condition remains true. The structure of `while` loops are very similar to the structure of `for` loops:

```
while x is true:
    Carry out action y
```

When we create a `while` loop, we need to create a variable that will be used to control the loop's execution. The loop will execute for as long as the variable we defined meets the condition we set. The `while` statement is conceptually simple, but it's important that when using a `while` loop you are sure to account for the potential problem of infinite loops. An infinite loop will occur if the value of the provided variable is never updated or if it always evaluated to True. If that's the case, then the loop will never finish, hence an infinite loop.

Here's a practical example of how to use the `while` statement:

```
value = 0

while value < 5:
    print("Part of the while loop")
    value = value + 1
else:
    print("The else condition")
```

6.6 - Recursion Vs. Iteration

Here's an important note on `for` loops and iterations: using a `for` loop to repeatedly run code until some end condition has been met is an iterative approach to solving a problem.

However, there's another method of tackling a problem that requires many of the same actions in a row. It's possible to create a function that calls itself and to have the function run continuously until it reaches the end criteria. Having a function call itself is called a "recursive" approach. You'll learn more about recursion later in this book. For now, know that there's another method of repeatedly carrying out a group of actions, but the iterative approach is Python's preferred approach. Python has a recursion limit that will prevent too many recursions from being carried out.

6.7 - Break/Continue

When you create `for` loops, sometimes you may want to end the loop early, stopping the loop when a certain criterion has been fulfilled, rather than iterating through the entire loop. The `break` keyword is utilized to end a loop early by exiting a loop and moving on to the next line in the program. Here's an example of how the `break` keyword can be used:

```
fruit_list = ['mango', 'lemon', 'banana', 'apple',
'cherry', 'watermelon', 'orange']

for fruit in fruit_list:
    print(fruit)
    if(fruit=='apple'):
        print("Apple is in the list")
        break

print("Loop ended")
```

The `break` command can be used to avoid situations where an infinite loop would otherwise occur. An infinite loop is kicked off if the loop never meets an end condition. One event where this might occur is if values are continually being added to a list and the loop is based on values that are currently in the list. In cases where `for` loops will not naturally come to an end, it's important that you use a `break` statement to end the loop.

Another keyword you should be aware of is the `continue` keyword, which can be used to skip the rest of the loop that follows the keyword.

Note that the code which follows the `continue` keyword will only be skipped if the `continue` criterion has been met. In other words, if the criterion used to trigger the `continue` evaluates as True, then the rest of the `for` loop will be skipped for that iteration. If in the next iteration, the `continue` criterion is not met, the loop will continue as normal.

Here's an example of the `continue` keyword in action:

```
print("Printing only odd numbers")
num_list = [24, 46, 21, 35, 62, 12, 19, 38, 20]
for i in num_list:
    if i%2 == 0:
        continue
    print(i)
```

6.8 - Try/Except

There are two final control flow statements to familiarize ourselves with, the `try` and `except` statements. These two statements are used in conjunction to control errors that may occur in your code. The `try` statement is used to specify what the computer should try, and the `except` statement is used to determine what should happen next if the operation cannot be carried out successfully. A `try`/`except` block can be set up like this:

```
try:
    Action to try
except:
    Do this instead
```

Here's a concrete example of how the `try`/`except` statements can be used:

```
value = input("Please enter a value to divide with:")
value = int(value)

try:
    numeric = 100//value
    print(numeric)
except:
    print("Error occurred, invalid value provided.")
```

The program prompts the user to input a value that will be used as a divisor. If the value provided is not something that can be divided into 100 (0), an error will occur, and the `except` part of the loop will be triggered. If this happens, the `try` block of the loop is ignored, and instead, the code under the `except` block runs. (If you enter a character that cannot be converted into a number, a different error will occur. Look at ValueError in the section below.

6.9 - Predefined Errors

While the `except` keyword is a general error keyword you can use, Python comes with many predefined error messages that are built-in. These unique error handlers can be used to control a variety of different possible errors, and they should trigger automatically when these associated error conditions occur. Here are some of Python's built-in error keywords and their use cases:

ValueError - Used when a value is of the incorrect type. For instance, it can be used when a value entered by the user needs to be converted into an integer, but the user has entered an incompatible string.

ZeroDivisionError - This error is triggered when trying to divide zero, which is impossible.

ImportError - This error is triggered when Python has been instructed to import a module, but the module cannot be found or otherwise cannot be imported successfully.

IOError - This Input/Output error notification occurs when an I/O operation cannot complete. For instance, this error would trigger when an `open()` command is called, but the provided file cannot be found.

Index Error - This IndexError occurs when a provided sequence index is out of the range of the sequence that has been provided.

KeyError - This error is triggered when a dictionary key is provided, but the provided key does not exist or can't be found within the dictionary.

TypeError - This error occurs when some function or operation has been applied to a data type but the operation cannot be carried out successfully.

NameError - This occurs when a designated variable name isn't found.

Each of the pre-defined errors has a pre-defined error message. The error messages can be displayed by setting the error as a variable and then printing the variable. As an example:

```
try:
    X = 1 / 0
except error as R:
    print(R)
```

When printing the error message, the generic variable Exception can be used to catch any errors not covered by the other error handlers.

6.10 - For Loops and Errors Exercise

We've covered a good amount of material so far, so let's take a moment to practice implementing the concepts we've learned over the last couple of chapters. Try to write a program that does the following:

- Creates a list or sequence
- Uses a `for` loop to iterate through the list and do something with the items in the list
- Breaks the `for` loop under some condition
- Includes some type of error handling

Below you'll find a possible solution for this exercise, but try to finish the exercise yourself before you look at the solution below.
Ready to see how this problem can be tackled? Go ahead and review the example below:

```python
num_list = [92, 11, 33, 59, 12, 65, 9, 43, 55, 1]

search_term = input("Enter a number to divide by:")

print("Starting loop")

for num in num_list:
    try:
        num = num//int(search_term)
        print(num)
    except:
        print("Incompatible divisor entered.")
        break

print("Loop ended")
```

Chapter 7:
Functions and Modules

Up until now, all the code we've looked at must be ran from top to bottom. We're now going to discuss how to create code blocks that, after they've been created, can be reused anywhere in the program. These bits of code are "functions" and "modules," and are extremely useful tools that can make your code much more efficient and quicker to write. We've briefly discussed modules and functions before, but we're now going to go over these concepts in greater detail and examine how you can implement them.

Let's take a moment to define some terms before moving forward. "Functions" are prewritten blocks of codes that can be invoked later to carry out the code within them. The variables and functions used in a script can be saved and exported, so that they may be used in other scripts and programs. When saved for later use, the file containing the functions is referred to as a "module." Since functions are used in the creation of modules, let's start by covering functions first.

7.1 - Functions

Functions are prewritten blocks of code that can be invoked to carry out a certain set of actions. You've been making use of a few different predefined functions in Python throughout this book, such as the `print()` function, which has Python take actions that result in the printing of a statement to the terminal. The `print()` function is a predefined Python function, but you'll soon learn how to write and use your own functions.

You can call functions in multiple ways. The most intuitive way of calling a function is to simply use the function name, followed by parentheses. Typing out the function name will typically invoke the function, although there is another way to call a function as well. You can also use "dot notation" to call a function. Using dot notation means placing a period before the name of the function, like this:

```
.function_name()
```

Dot notation is used to tell Python you want to call a function on a specific object, with the name of the object coming just before the period, like this:

```
target_object.function_name()
```

Sometimes when we call a function, we need to provide the function with certain variables or data values. These values that we give to the function for it to use are called "parameters" or "arguments." The parameters or arguments are passed to the function by putting them within a set of parentheses that follows the function name. When passing multiple arguments to a function, separate the individual arguments with commas.

By now, you should be familiar with one example of passing arguments to a function, just consider how you've used the `print()` function before.

```
print("This string value is being passed into the
function call as an argument")
```

If the function requires two or more arguments, you would simply pass in multiple arguments separated by commas.

7.2 - Creating Your Own Functions

Let's learn how to create our own functions and make use of them within other scripts and programs. In order to tell Python that you would like to create a function, you can use the `def` keyword. The `def` keyword tells Python you want to define a function and that it needs to recognize a variety of keywords and values to follow. After using the `def` keyword, you need to provide the function name and any arguments/parameters your function will make use of. You can then begin writing the commands you'd like your function to carry out. In other words, the syntax for creating a function looks something like this:

```
def name(parameters):
    Code to carry out desired actions
```

Your functions will often require another keyword, the `return` keyword. The `return` keyword specifies an expression, variable, or value you'd like the function to pass back out to the main program once the function has finished running. Once the return statement is executed, the function will stop running, and the expression you've designated will be passed back. Here's how to return an expression or value:

```
def name(parameters):
    Code to carry out desired actions
    return desiredExpression
```

If your function returns a value, you can assign that value to a variable by calling the function and assigning it to a variable. You can then manipulate the return value that has been stored in the variable.

```
returned_value = function_used(list of parameters)
```

If your function does not need to return a value, you can either just not use the `return` keyword or use `return None`.

66

Here's an example of a function that you can run in PyCharm:

```python
def multiply_values(num_1, num_2):
    num_3 = 2
    print("Number 1 is : " + str(num_1))
    print("Number 2 is : " + str(num_2))
    print("Number 3 is: " + str(num_3))
    mult_num = num_1 * num_2 * num_3
    print("Product  of  multiplication  is:  " +
str(mult_num))
    return mult_num
```

The function takes in two different numbers as parameters, multiplies these numbers together, and then multiplies the product of those numbers by two. The function then returns the multiplied value. The function also prints out the numerical values that have been passed in, as well as the product of the multiplication.

We can now call the function, assign it to a variable, and then print the variable to make sure that the returned value is what we expect it to be.

```python
multiplied = multiply_values(8, 9)
print(multiplied)
```

You may notice that we have called the `print` function within our own function. Python allows you to call functions within functions like this, even your own custom functions.

7.3 - Variable Scope

We've worked quite a bit with variables thus far, but now we need to take some time to discuss an important aspect of variables – "variable scope."

Variable scope refers to the visibility or accessibility of variables. When you look through a telescope at a landscape, you can only see objects that the telescope is directed at. Similarly, variables can only be used by Python if they are in the correct scope, and if the program can see the variable at the current point in time.

Variables declared inside a function are a part of that function's scope, and they are handled differently than variables created outside the scope of the function. The difference is that variables created within a function can only be used inside that function; they are not accessible by the program at large. Meanwhile, variables declared outside the function are "global" in scope, and they can be accessed by the entire program. Global variables stand in contrast to local variables (those created within a function).

We can understand the scope better if we look at the function we defined above. Trying to access and print out the variable num_3 will cause an error, as it is local to the function and not accessible by the rest of the program. For this reason, a NameError is thrown. However, if we declare a new variable (num_4) outside the function, this variable is global and can be printed. If you wanted to, you could pass num_4 to the function when you call it, and the function would be able to use it as it is a global variable.

```python
def multiply_values(num_1, num_2):
    num_3 = 2
    print("Number 1 is : " + str(num_1))
    print("Number 2 is : " + str(num_2))
    print("Number 3 is: " + str(num_3))
    mult_num = num_1 * num_2 * num_3
    print("Product   of   multiplication   is:   "   +
str(mult_num))
    return mult_num
```

```
multiplied = multiply_values(8, 9)
print(multiplied)

num_4 = 12
print(num_4)

# Attempting to run this will cause an error
print(num_3)
```
It's important to understand that if you have a function variable/local variable that matches the name of a global variable, the function will not reference the global variable. In other words, if a local variable and global variable have the same name, the function uses the local variable and not the global variable. However, any code written outside of the function will reference the global variable.

7.4 - Default Parameters

We've covered functions and variable scope, which are the basics of functions. Now we can start getting into the more subtle usages and options for functions in Python.

Python allows you to specify default values for parameters that will be used in a function. Default values are useful because they enable the program to run without needing to pass values for all the parameters at run time. In order to create default values in a function, you can use the assignment operator to assign a default value when initially creating the function.

```
def sample_function(variable_1, variable_2 = 9):
    print("Variable 1 is: " + str(variable_1))
    print("variable 2 is: " + str(variable_2))

sample_function(12)
```

69

Running the code above, you'll discover that the value for `variable_1` is 12, as specified when the function is called. However, the value for `variable_2` is 9, as there was no value passed in for it and 9 was the default value. If a function has defaulted parameters, the defaulted parameters must be at the end of the list. You cannot write a function that has defaulted parameters defined in the middle or at the beginning of the list of function parameters.

Just because the function above has a default value does not mean we have to keep using the default value. We can overwrite the default value simply by passing in a value for the second parameter when it is called.
`sample_function(12, 24)`

As you can see, overwriting the default function value is very simple. Just remember that the values you pass into the function are assigned to the parameters in the order that the parameters are defined. If you wanted `variable_2` to have a value of 19 and not 12, you need to make sure the value 19 is passed second.

7.5 - Variable-Length Arguments - Lists and Keywords (*args and **kwargs)

Thus far, we've created functions where we know, in advance, the number of variables we will need within the scope of the function. However, what can we do if we don't know how many arguments a function will need? Python allows us to handle situations like this by using variable-length argument lists and keyword argument dictionaries.

You can think of using variable-length argument lists as passing an empty list into the function, a list that will be filled in with values as the program is running. (Variable-length arguments aren't perfectly synonymous with lists, but for illustrative purposes, this is good enough.)

Let's assume you have a database full of sentences, and you need to print out the sentences. However, you don't know how many sentences there are in the database. A function that allows you to do this, using variable-length arguments, would look like this:

```
def print_sentences(*sentences):
    for sentence in sentences:
        print(sentence)
```

The advantage of using a function like this is that you can just add sentences straight to the function call as parameters, without having to alter the way your function works in any way. You simply use the asterisk symbol (*) to tell Python that it should be prepared to work with an unknown number of arguments passed in as a list.

```
print_sentences(sentence_1, sentence_2, sentence_3)
```

Essentially, the asterisk declares that a list of items that will vary in length will be passed to the function. We can also do the same with keywords instead of non-keyword argument lists. In order to use a variable-length keyword dictionary, we declare the argument dictionary with two asterisks instead of one (**).

Assume that we have a large dictionary of contact information, containing names and email addresses. We want to print out both the key (name) and the value (email address). We can accomplish this by writing a function that looks something like this:

```
def print_emails(**emails):
    for name, email in emails.items():
        print("Name = {}, email = {}".format(name, email)
```

71

We can then use our function by calling it and passing in the names and emails in keyword assignment format (email_1 = "test@email.com").

```
print_emails('Dictionary information here')
```

For the sake of clarity, the functions above were written with `sentences` and `emails`, as the names of the variable-length argument lists and keyword dictionaries. However, the names could potentially be anything. That said, when you use these concepts in your own code, you are encouraged to stick to Python convention and use `*args` (arguments) and `**kwargs` (keyword arguments) as their names.

One more thing to note when making use of `*args` and `**kwargs`. If your function utilizes any combination of regular arguments, `*args`, and `**kwargs`, the parameters must be declared within the parentheses in a specific order. The regular argument must come first, then the `*args`, and finally the `**kwargs`.

7.6 - Importing Modules

Let's look at how to use some of Python's built-in functions. We've already gone over some of Python's included functions, like the `print()` function. These functions are part of the standard Python package. In contrast, some additional functions come with a Python installation but aren't available for use until you `import` them. Such functions are referred to as "modules."

In order to import a module, you can use one of several different import methods. The entire module can be imported by simply typing:

```
import name_of_module
```

For example, Python comes with a module called random, which can be used to generate random numbers. To import this module, you would just type:

```
import random
```

When you import a module with the above method, in order to use a function that the module possesses, you need to call the function using dot notation. For example, in order to make use of the randrange() function, you can use the following syntax:

```
random_nums = random.randrange(0, 25)
```

You can also assign shorthand or nicknames to a module that you import so that you don't have to write out the name of the module each time. For instance, we can alias random like this:

```
import random as r
```

We can now call the randrange function simply by writing:

```
random_nums2 = r.randrange(0, 25)
```

We can also import specific functions rather than importing an entire module. We can import specific functions by specifying the name of the module with `from` and then using the `import` keyword with the name of the functions we want to import.

```
from random import randrange
```

Importing a specific function this way enables us to just refer to the function by name when we want to use it:

```
random_nums3 = randrange(0, 25)
```

You can import multiple functions from a module by separating the name of the functions you wish to import with a comma. In general, if you don't need to use many functions from the module, it's a good idea to import just the functions you need rather than the entire module.

7.7 - Creating Modules

After you create your own functions, you can package them into modules for use in other programs and scripts. Creating modules out of functions that you commonly use may save you a lot of time, as you can just reuse them for future projects. Python makes it very easy to create a module and import it to another program; all you must do is the following:

- Make sure that the file you created the function in is saved in the ".py" extension.
- Ensure that the file containing the function is in the same folder as the file you are importing the function to.

Here's a practical example of how to do that. Let's say we're creating a function that will join multiple input phrases into a single string. The function might look something like this:

```
def args_to_string(*args):
    string_1 = ""

    for i in args:
        string_1 += i + " "

    return string_1
```

We can save the function in a file called `argtostring.py` and after that, we can create another file in the same directory using PyCharm. Next, we import the function for use.

```
from argtostring import args_to_string

string_1 = args_to_string('Hello,', 'this', 'should',
'be', 'one', 'string.')
print(string_1)
```

While using an imported function in the same directory is that simple, you may have to use a function that is in a different directory. We'll discuss navigating files and directories later in this book, but here's a quick look at how you can access a file that is in a different directory. You can use the `sys` module, which enables Python to change where it searches for files. Let's assume that the file you created was stored in a folder called `PythonPrograms` saved on the C drive. In this case, you could simply use the `sys` module to include that folder as part of the "path," the list of directories that Python will search when looking for files.

```
import sys
sys.path.append('C:\\PythonPrograms')
```

Including these commands in your program would be enough for Python to be able to find the `argtostring.py` file stored there.

7.8 - Useful Built-In Functions and Methods

By now, you've seen that using functions can save you a huge amount of time and energy. Therefore, it will pay off to know about some commonly used Python functions. The functions listed below are all built-in to Python and can be called simply by invoking them with no imports needed. Also included in this section are methods, which act like functions, but only work on specific data types and structures. The methods are typically invoked using dot notation on the target object.

`print()` - We've already covered this extensively, but it prints out the provided arguments to your terminal or screen.

`abs()` - This returns the absolute value of the provided argument, assuming the value is a numerical value (a float or integer).

`round()` - Rounds the provided numerical value to the nearest integer.

`min()` - Finds and returns the smallest value in a list of values. It even works on strings, where it will select the earliest alphabetical characters.

`max()` - The opposite of min, finds the largest or alphabetically last values.

`sorted()` - Sorts a list in ascending order and works on both numerical values and strings.

`sum()` - Adds the elements of a list together and returns the sum.

`len()` - Counts and returns the number of elements in a list. If called on a string, it will return the number of characters in the string.

`type()` - Returns the data type of the variable that the function has been provided.

String Methods

`lower()` - Converts all elements of the string to lowercase.

`upper()` - Converts all elements of the string to uppercase.

`strip()` - Removes extra whitespace from the beginning or end of the string.

`replace()` - Takes two arguments and replaces the first string with the second string.

`split()` - Takes in a specified delimiter as an argument and splits the string on that delimiter (splits strings into a list, splitting whenever the specified character occurs).

`join()` - Joins elements of a list into a single string, and you can choose the delimiter to join on.

List Methods
`append()` - Adds the provided argument to a list.

`remove()` - Removes the provided argument from a list.

`count()` - Returns the index number of the given value in a list.

`clear()` - Removes all elements from a list.

Dictionary Methods

`keys()` - Gives all the keys found in the dictionary.

`values()` - Gives all the values found in the dictionary.

`clear()` - Deletes everything from the dictionary.

7.9 - Functions and Imports Exercise

Functions are an incredibly important part of programming in Python, so let's be sure that we understand them before moving on to the next topic.

We'll try another programming exercise, and this time, we will focus on functions and imports.

Try doing the following:

- Write a function that takes arguments and manipulates the values of those arguments in some way (bonus points for making use of *args or **kwargs). Return the results of the manipulation. Use local variables in the function.
- Save the file your function is in within your current folder.
- Create a new file.
- Import the function from your original file.
- Create some global variables and pass them into the function.
- Print the resulting value of the function.

After you've attempted this by yourself, you can review the example below to see one way of meeting the requirements for this exercise.

Here's one potential solution:

```python
# save this in a file called "shopping_list.py"
def shopping_list(store, *args):

    shopping_list = []

    for i in args:
        print("Adding {} to list".format(i))
        shopping_list.append(str(store)  +  "  -  "  +
str(i))

    return shopping_list
```

In another file in the same directory:

```
# create a new file in the same directory (or alias
the import)

from shopping_list import shopping_list as SL

grocery_list = SL("Hilltop Grocery", "bread", "milk",
"coffee", "apple juice")
computer_list = SL("Top Computer Parts", "RAM",
"keyboard", "USB hub")
print(grocery_list)
print(computer_list)
```

Chapter 8:
Object-Oriented Programming
Part 1 - Classes and Instances

The following two chapters will delve into one of the most essential programming ideas in Python: object-oriented programming.

This chapter will serve as an introduction to the idea of object-oriented-programming, explaining what classes are and how they are constructed, while the chapter after will look at more advanced features of classes.

8.1 - What are Classes?

Object-oriented programming refers to a programming paradigm (a philosophy of programming) that aims to break down complex problems into simple objects that interact with one another. In Python, the blueprint that objects are built from is known as a "class," while the actual item that is instantiated with these blueprints is the "object."

Classes are the blueprints for objects that we can use when writing programs. Classes, and the actual objects they will become, have two important components: "attributes" and "methods." You can think of attributes as the characteristics of the class, analogous to variables in a function. Meanwhile, methods are like functions themselves, actions that the object can take (ways we can interact with that object).

To make this more concrete, let's think about a real-world example of an instance we can create a class in. Let's say we oversee employee documentation for a company. We want to create a class that represents employees, tracks their attributes, and allows us to update their attributes.

To accomplish this, we would create an `Employee` class, a blueprint that will allow us to create individual objects representing individual employees. The employee class will contain attributes like name, role, email, etc., and it will also have a variety of methods that we can use to update their role should they shift jobs within the company.

The advantage of creating a class that we can use as a blueprint is that we don't have to create a dictionary for each employee from scratch.

8.2 - Creating Classes

Let's look at how we can create classes. To create a class in Python, we simply use the `class` keyword to begin writing a class, followed by the name of the class we want to create. (Class names are encouraged to be in CamelCase, with the first letter of each word capitalized.)

```
class Employee:
    pass
```

Above is how we would create an Employee class, and if you're not sure of what attributes or methods you want the class to include, you can just write the keyword `pass`, which will have Python recognize it as a valid class that currently does nothing.

The next thing we need to do to get our class up and running is initialize the class. We do this with a constructor or `init` method. The init method will pass in the attributes we want the class to have, but before we do that, we need to pass in `self`. Why do we need to pass in a self argument to the initialization method? You can think of it as the initialization method asking what arguments it should create an instance of, and naturally, the class must construct an instance of itself. We can then go on to specify other attributes that we would like the class to have. When we create the attributes, we need to specify `self` for the individual attributes in the init method and then assign the values that will be passed to the object when it's created.

```
class Employee:
    def __init__(self, name, email, role):
        self.name = name
        self.email = email
        self.role = role
```

Now that the class has been created, we can go about instantiating an actual object using the class blueprint. We'll create an object by calling the class, much like how we call a function, and assigning that to a variable. We pass in arguments consisting of the values we want the class to use, and we need to be sure we pass the arguments in the order they appear above in the init method. We do not need to specify "self" as that value is used in the constructor call by default.

```
employee_1 = Employee("E. Davis",
"edavis@business.com", "Hiring Manager")
employee_2 = Employee("D. Wong", "dwong@business.com",
"Developer")
```

After we've created an instance of the class, we can access the individual elements of the class and update them. We access the desired attribute using dot notation and update the value of an attribute simply by assigning it a new value. After creating the class and objects from the class using the code above, add the code below to the script and run it to see how things change.

```
print(employee_1.role)
employee_1.role = "Lead developer"
print(employee_1.role)
```

8.3 - Class Variables and Instance Variables

When we discussed functions, we distinguished global variables and function/local variables. The difference between these was called scope. Classes and the objects that are created with the class blueprints can also have different variable scopes. In this case, the difference can be described as class variables vs. instance variables.

A class variable is a variable that belongs to the entire class and each instance created with that class will share that class variable. For example, let's say we update the class blueprint we created to include another variable, but place the variable outside a method under the main scope of the class.

```
class Employee:

    location = "Seattle, WA"

    def __init__(self, name, email, role):
        self.name = name
        self.email = email
        self.role = role
```

We have created a variable outside the constructor method, and this means that the variable applies to all instances of the class that are created. If we had placed the variable inside the init method and used self, it would mean that every instance created with the class would have its unique location. Instead, as a class variable, it applies to all instances, reflecting that all the employees are in one physical location.

We can try creating instances of the class and print out their location. Notice how they are the same.

```
employee_1          =          Employee("E.          Davis",
"edavis@business.com", "Hiring Manager")
employee_2 = Employee("D. Wong", "dwong@business.com",
"Developer")

print(employee_1.location)
print(employee_2.location)
```

As for the instance variables, we've already seen how these are used. The instance variables are unique to each instance of the class, and they are passed in as arguments when the class is created.

In summary, here's a quick breakdown of the differences between class and instance variables:

- Class variables are created outside of any method, and they can be accessed outside of the class by using the name of the class. Altering the value of a class variable will change the value in all instances of the class.
- Instance variables are created within a method of the class, and they must be created with `self`. They must be accessed using the name of the instance, not the class, and altering the value of an instance variable will only impact that specific instance.

8.4 - Class Methods and Static Methods

Since we now know how to create classes and attributes, we can discuss how to create "methods." Methods are basically functions that belong to a class. They are used to carry out specific tasks, but they can only be used directly on an object that has been created using the class blueprint.

Let's try adding a method to the class we created above that can be used to print out the name, email, and role of an instance, all with one method.

We define a method in a class much like how we define functions, with the `def` keyword and then the arguments the method takes. Similar to the `init` method, every method within a class will take the instance as the first argument, so we need to pass `self` first.

```
class Employee:

    location = "Seattle, WA"

    def __init__(self, name, email, role):
        self.name = name
        self.email = email
        self.role = role

    def get_info(self):
        return '{} {} {}'.format(self.name,
self.email, self.role)
```

Creating a method like this will enable us to get all the relevant info just by calling the method on our object instance of the class in a print statement. Note that we're returning the info in the code above, so when we choose to print out the info, we need to wrap the method call in a `print` statement.

```
employee_1          =          Employee("E.          Davis",
"edavis@business.com", "Hiring Manager")
employee_2 = Employee("D. Wong", "dwong@business.com",
"Developer")

print(employee_1.get_info())
```

We can also use an alternate way of calling our method, calling it directly on the class, and then passing in the desired instance.

```
print(Employee.get_info(employee_1))
```

Much like how there is more than one kind of variables when it comes to classes (class and instance variables), there are also more than one kind of class methods. There are regular (instance) methods, class methods, and static methods. The type of method we've discussed above is an instance method. It applies to an instance of the class and is the most common method type used.

Python also makes use of class and static methods. In all likelihood, you won't use either class or static methods anywhere near as often as you use the regular, instance methods. In order to create the class and static methods, we use what is referred to as a decorator. The decorator starts with an @ symbol, like this - @staticmethod or @classmethod. It is placed directly above the line containing the def keyword that starts the method.

Class methods take in classes as the first parameter instead of the self keyword, and this is usually represented by cls. The keyword cls is used to specify an entire class rather than an instance. If an instance (regular) method accesses instance variables, you might be able to guess that the primary use of class methods is to access and manipulate the class variables you have created within a class. For example, using a class method, we can change the location class variable we created above.

Below, we'll create a class method that operates on the class. We use the @classmethod decorator and pass in cls as the first argument. We then update the class location to a new location we pass in when we call the method. We'll create a new employee to test the new class method.

```
class Employee:
    location = "Seattle, WA"
```

```python
    def __init__(self, name, email, role):
        self.name = name
        self.email = email
        self.role = role

    def get_info(self):
        return '{} {} {}'.format(self.name,
self.email, self.role)

    @classmethod
    def change_locale(cls, new_location):
        cls.location = new_location

employee_3 = Employee("R. Acevedo",
"racevedo@business.com", "Developer")

print(employee_3.location)
Employee.change_locale('Los Angeles, CA')
print(employee_3.location)
```

Python also has another form of method: the static method. Static methods are methods that receive neither an instance nor a class when they are called. Static methods are bound to a class instead of an object, and they deal with parameters of the class. Since static methods can't access the properties of the class itself, they have limited use cases. Static methods are typically only used when a utility function is required that doesn't operate on any properties of a class, but still makes sense for the method to belong to the class.

Chapter 9:
Object-Oriented Programming
Part 2 - Inheritance, Child Classes, and Special Methods

9.1 - Inheritance

In part two of our discussion regarding object-oriented programming, we're going to cover the concept of inheritance. Inheritance is one of the most essential concepts in object-oriented programming because it allows the reuse of existing code. Thanks to inheritance, we don't need to write an entire class from scratch. If we have one class that has a particular functionality and structure, and we would like to copy aspects of that class, we can just inherit from that particular class.

To make sense of inheritance, let's think about the definition of the word. If you think about the word in a biological context, you might think about a child inheriting traits from a parent. The parent's traits are passed down to the child, and they become parts of that child's traits. That's also what happens with inheritance in Python classes. The class that contains the desired trait is called the "parent" class, while the class that receives the trait is called the "child" class (or the base class). A child class is a subclass that can potentially use all the variables and methods of the parent class, which means these methods and attributes don't have to be rewritten.

For us to see how this works, let's start by creating a new class. We declare the class with the `class` keyword just like normal, but we will also pass in an argument of Employee. This signals to Python that we want to inherit from the Employee class and that this Developer class will be a child of the Employee class.

When we get to the init method, we're going to want to pass in every attribute we want the class to use, both new and old attributes. For this reason, we pass in all the old attributes plus a new attribute we will call language. After this, all we have to do to let the Employee class handle the logic behind the old attributes is to use the super() function (note that you don't have to pass in self when using super()), followed by another init method, and the attributes we want to inherit. Finally, we just add in the new attribute we want, just as we did in our previous class.

```
class Employee:

    location = "Seattle, WA"

    def __init__(self, name, email, role):
        self.name = name
        self.email = email
        self.role = role

    def get_info(self):
        return '{} {} {}'.format(self.name,
self.email, self.role)

class Developer (Employee):

    def __init__(self, name, email, role, language):
        super().__init__(name, email, role)
        self.language = language

    def get_info(self):
        return '{} {} {}'.format(self.name,
self.email, self.role)
```

Let's try switching our previous Employee objects to instances of the Developer class and passing in a language for them to use.

```
employee_1 = Developer("E. Davis",
"edavis@business.com", "Lead Developer", "Python")
employee_2 = Developer("D. Wong",
"dwong@business.com", "Developer", "Python")
```

Let's try printing some of the info now.

```
print(employee_1.email)
print(employee_2.language)
```

You can now see that the Employee class is handling the email attribute while the Developer is correctly handling the language attribute. Language only exists within the subclass/child class, not the Employee class.

You can also inherit methods from a parent class. For instance, if we were to create a new class and wanted to inherit our `get_info` method from our old Employee class, all we would need to do is use `super()` followed by the name of our chosen method in dot notation:

```
super().get_info()
```

That would be enough to call the parent function, and we could do whatever we wanted with it, like assign it to a variable. A parent method has access to all the variables from the parent class by default. However, if we wanted a method that interacted with the `language` attribute, we'd have to create a new one. If we created a new method in the child class with the same name as the parent class, the functionality of the new method would override the old method.

Classes can be difficult for beginners to understand, but with enough time and practice, you will make sense of them. It's highly recommended that you try creating your own classes and experiment with them, getting a feel for things like instance vs. class variables and inheritance.

If you are ever confused about if an object is an instance of a class or a subclass, Python has convenient ways to check. You can use the `isinstance()` and `issubclass()` to check if objects are instances of subclasses. `isinstance()` takes an object and the class in question as arguments, while `issubclass()` takes the names of two classes, checking to see if the first class is a subclass of the second.

Try the code below to see that Python has identified employee_1 as an instance of the Developer class(it is also an instance of the employee class because it inherits from it), and Developer as a subclass of Employee. The print statements will be "True" for the examples below, but if you swapped Employee and Developer in the second print statement, you would get "False" instead.

```
print(isinstance(employee_1, Developer))
print(issubclass(Developer, Employee))
```

9.2 - Multiple Inheritance

It's possible to inherit from multiple classes. In order to do so, you need to specify the parent classes in the class creation statement and specify what attributes you want to inherit when you initialize the child class. Remember that, by default, the child class will have access to the methods of both parent classes.

Let's say we wanted to create a new `Equipment` class that will keep track of what equipment the employees are using and who owns that piece of equipment. After we create the class, we can update our `Developer` class to inherit from the new `Equipment` class. We'll then

91

just create a few `Equipment` objects and pass them in as arguments when we create our Developer objects.

```
class Equipment:

    def __init__(self, type, owner):
        self.type = type
        self.owner = owner

    def show_equipment(self):
        return '{} - Owned By: {}'.format(self.type,
self.owner)

class Developer (Employee, Equipment):

    def __init__(self, name, email, role, type, owner,
language):
        super().__init__(name, email, role)
        self.type = type
        self.owner = owner
        self.language = language

    def get_info(self):
        return '{} {} {}'.format(self.name,
self.email, self.role)

equipment_1 = Equipment("Desktop", "Company")
equipment_2 = Equipment("Laptop", "D. Wong")
```

Now we just create new employee objects and pass in the equipment values as arguments. We can then use the `show_equipment` method we defined in our `Equipment` class.

```
employee_1 = Developer("E. Davis",
"edavis@business.com", "Lead Developer",
equipment_1.type, equipment_1.owner, "Python")

employee_2 = Developer("D. Wong",
"dwong@business.com", "Developer", equipment_2.type,
equipment_2.owner, "Python")

print(employee_1.show_equipment())
print(employee_2.show_equipment())
```

9.3 - Importing Classes

Much like you can import functions into a Python file, you can also import classes. To do this, Python needs to have access to the directory that holds the file that defines the classes, much like with functions. Once Python has access to the file, there are multiple ways to import classes.

You can import the entire file and then use the target class by using parentheses:

```
import classfile

class_object = classfile.TargetClass()
```

If you don't want to have to prefix the class name with the name of the file, you can import the class directly with the from keyword.

```
from classfile import TargetClass

class_object = TargetClass()
```

9.4 - Python Special Methods

Before we wrap up our discussion of classes and object-oriented programming, let's talk about Python's special methods. Special methods allow us to override some of Python's built-in behavior and operations. Special methods are also referred to as "magic methods" or "dunder method" (short for "double underscore," because of the way that they are written, with two underscores on both sides of the method name). We've already seen this format with the `init` method we use to initialize a class:

```
__init__
```

The `init` method is just one example of a special method. There are two more common special methods you might see, and it's a good idea to use them when creating your classes. These methods are `__repr__` and `__str__`. These two methods control how your class object will be displayed. The `__repr__` method is intended to be used as a clear description of the object for other developers, while the `__str__` method is intended to be used to provide descriptions to end-users.

When you use the `__repr__` method, it's a good idea to return a description that another developer could use to recreate your object. For instance, if we were to write a `__repr__` method for the Developer class we created in the previous chapters, it might look something like the following:

```
def __repr__(self):
    return                  "Employee('{}',                  '{}',
'{}')".format(self.name, self.email, self.role)
```

The return value of the `__repr__` method will be printed out to the terminal if the `print()` function is used on an object of the class. For example, after inserting that method into our employee class, we can use the following print statement:

```
print(employee_1)
```

The __repr__ method can also be invoked like a function:

```
print(repr(employee_1))
```

Both methods should give us something like this:

```
Developer("E.   Davis",   "edavis@business.com",   "Lead
Developer", "Python")
```

This would give other developers an intuitive sense of how they could recreate that object or create other similar objects. You can set up your __str__ method in a similar way, but design it to provide feedback that might be more useful for the end-user.

Python has several other magic/special methods you can use to alter how it handles specific conditions. For example, there are mathematical methods you can use to alter what occurs when mathematical operators are used. These methods include: __add__, __sub__, __mul__, and __div__. They operate on +, -, *, and, or respectively. You can visit the website below to check the documentation and see many other numeric special   methods. (https://docs.python.org/3/reference/datamodel.html#emulating-numeric-types)

One use case for these special mathematical methods is when trying to allow the user to add the numerical values of attributes together. If the Employee class has a Pay attribute, you can allow another developer to get the total pay for two or more combined Employee objects by creating

95

an __add__ special method that adds together the `self.pay` and `other.pay` values. Once the method is created, what the developer needs to do is create a variable and join the two objects along with the addition operator (+).

9.5 - Classes and Methods Exercise

Let's take some time to make sure that we understand classes and methods before we move on to other topics. It's important to be comfortable with classes, as they are a significant part of programming in Python. Let's do another exercise before we move on to other topics. Try writing a program that does the following:

- Creates a class with various attributes
- Creates a method or two within the class that alters or displays the attributes
- Creates a second class that inherits attributes from the first class
- Creates a new attribute in the second class
- Instantiates an object created from the second/child class
- Uses the method(s) you created in the parent class on the object created from the child class

Give that a shot before looking below for an idea of how this can be accomplished.

Ready to see a solution now? Go for it:

```
class Dog:

    breed = "Labrador"

    def __init__(self, name, color):
        self.name = name
```

```python
        self.color = color

    @classmethod
    def change_breed(cls, new_breed):
        cls.breed = new_breed

class Puppy(Dog):
    def __init__(self, color, name, age):
        super().__init__(self, color)
        self.color = color
        self.name = name
        self.age = age

    def display_info(self):
        return 'Breed: {} - Color: {} - Name: {} -
Age: {}'.format(self.breed, self.color, self.name,
self.age)

dog_1 = Dog("Sally", "Black")
print(dog_1.breed)

dog_2 = Puppy("Brown", "Kaylee", "3 months")
print(dog_2.display_info())

dog_2.change_breed("Corgi")
print(dog_2.breed)
```

Chapter 10:
Files

In this chapter, we'll discuss working with files. Often during your programming journey, you'll want to pull in data from external files and manipulate that data. For example, maybe you have a large word document, but you only want sentences that contain certain words and phrases. With Python, you can read the document, do a search for the desired strings, join these strings into a list, and write a new document containing just the target strings. Python has many built-in functions and features that make loading, reading, and even writing to external files simple. Let's see the various ways we can interact with a file using Python.

10.1 Opening and Reading

To begin our exploration of files, we'll first need a text file to work with. Copy any text you'd like into a text editor and save it to the same directory as your Python scripts, saving it with the ".txt" format. If you need text to work with, you can try writing the following and running the script:

import this

Running this script will activate a Python Easter Egg, printing out the Zen of Python (a list of the principles that guide design in Python). If you would like, you can copy that text into a text file and save it.

To open a file in Python, we can use the `open()` function, which takes two arguments. The first argument is the file that you want to open, while the second argument specifies the mode that the file will be opened in.

For example, if you have a folder called "Projects" on your C drive, you would have to specify that Python looks for the targeted file by passing in: `C:\\Projects\\test_text.txt`.

With this in mind, you can assign the contents of a file to a variable by doing this:

```
text_file = open("text_test.txt", "r")
```

The first argument specifies where Python should look for the file that you want to open. If the file is in the same directory as the program you are writing, all you need to do is provide the name and extension of the file. If this isn't the case and the file is located elsewhere, you'll need to provide the full path to the file, as mentioned above.

In the case above, the `r` specifies that we want to open the document in read-only mode. The other file-handling options include:

`w` mode - Specifies you want to open the file in write-only mode.
`w` will create the file that has been passed in as the first argument if the file doesn't already exist. Be careful when using this, because the data in the file will be erased if the file already exists.

`a` mode – Used for opening the file in appending-mode. Appending is for adding text to the current body of the file. If the file doesn't exist yet, the file will be created. Unlike `w`, the existing data in the file isn't erased if the file already exists. This is because any new data is added to the end of the file.

`r+` - Specifies that you want to both read and write to the file.

After you have created a file object by using the `open()` function and the `assignment` operator, it's possible to read out individual lines in the document by using the `readline()` function, which is done by using dot notation on the file object:

```
text_file.readline()
```

Each time the `readline()` function is called, it moves to the next line in the text document. This means that if you call the function and print the results three times, Python will print out the first three lines in the document.

A more efficient way of printing out multiple lines from a file is by using a `for` loop. We can easily print out all the lines in a text file by writing a statement like:

```
for i in text_file:
    print(i)
```

Now that you know how to open files in Python, you should also know how to close them. You can close a file you've opened simply by using the `close()` function on it, like this:

```
text_file.close()
```

You should get in the habit of closing files after you are done working with them, because this frees up resources your system is using to keep the file open.

10.2 - Writing to Text Files

Let's learn how to write text to a file in Python. For us to accomplish this, we can use either the `a` or `w` modes, but if we use `w`, the current content of our text file will be erased whenever our program runs. For this reason, it's often smarter to write to files in a/append mode. Writing to a file in

Python can be accomplished using the intuitively named `write()` function. The function merely takes in the text you want to write as an argument and is invoked with dot notation on the text file object you've created. We could create and write to a text file by doing this:

```
target_file = open("write_test.txt", "a")

# \n creates a new line
target_file.write("All we have to do is type in a
sentence to write to the document. \n")
target_file.write("Using the write function multiple
times will write multiples lines to the document. \n")
```

Much like we can use a `for` loop to read from a text document, we can also use a `for` loop to write to a text document. We could make a list full of strings to write and then use a `for` loop to write to the document, which would write our list items on different lines.

```
list_to_write = ["This", " is", " our", " word", "
list"]

for w in list_to_write:
    target_file.write(w)

target_file.close()
```

Remember that you can format how your string is written into the text document by using the escape character and formatting options we discussed in the chapter on string formatting.

10.3 - Buffer Size/Binary Files

When you first start writing your programs, you'll probably only be working with small text files that don't take up a lot of memory. However, when you start to work with larger collections of data and bigger text files, you'll want to know how to specify a buffer size. Buffering our file allows us to read it in small chunks, so that it doesn't take up too much memory. Python will divide the text document up, reading it in by the specified buffer size. We can declare the desired buffer size by using the `read()` function and passing in the buffer size as an argument.

When we pass in the buffer size, Python expects a numerical value. We are specifying the number of bytes to read at one time. Let's say we wanted to read our test text file 20 bytes at a time.

```
text = open("test_text.txt", "r")
print(text.read(20))
```

Printing the text variable would now display the first 20 bytes of the text document. If you wanted to loop through the entire document, you would need to use a `while` loop, setting the end condition as the length of the file, and then updating the current value of the text variable by using the function again to get the next 20 bytes. After opening the file, try running the code below and notice it prints out the text file in blocks of 20 bytes.

```
text = target_file.read(20)

while len(text):
    print(text)
    text = target_file.read(20)
```

Python interprets non-text files in binary, so the term "binary file" describes non-text files (as opposed to ASCII or other human-readable file encodings). We can work with these non-text files by using specific modes that let the `open()` function know we want to read or write binary: `rb` and `wb`. If you were aiming to open an image file and copy it over to another file, this could be done simply by opening an image file with the mode set to `rb` and then copy the lines of data over by opening a new file with the mode set to `wb`.

10.4 - Deleting and Renaming

There are two other functions that you should be aware of when working with files in Python. The `remove()` function and `rename()` function help you deal with files in a folder, either by deleting the files or renaming the files. These are part of the `os` library, so this means that the functions will need to be imported before they can be used.

```
from os import remove, rename
```

This `remove()` function takes the name of the target file as its only parameter, so the syntax looks like this:

```
remove(target_file)
```

Meanwhile, the `rename()` function takes in two arguments, the current name of the target file and the name you wish to rename the file to.

```
rename("old_filename.txt","new_filename.txt")
```

Chapter 11:
Intermediate and Advanced Concepts

If you've gotten this far, you've covered the basics and gone over most of what you'll need to know to start writing programs in Python. You should feel proud of yourself for making it this far. For the rest of this book, we'll be going into more intermediate and advanced Python concepts with a large project at the very end. From here, we'll start covering topics like lambda functions, packages, virtual environments, image manipulation, regular expressions, and unit testing.

11.1 - Recursion

Whenever you need to work with a sequence of data, you must traverse through the sequence somehow. You already know how to do this with `for` loops. Constructing a for loop and carrying out some action until a stopping condition is met is known as an iterative approach to working with sequential data. However, there's another method of working with data sequences: you can also create a recursive function.

Python allows you to write functions that call themselves within their function definition. The term "recursion" is applied in any instance where a function calls itself. Recursion will continue to carry out the actions specified within the function until an end condition is met. Most iterative functions can be written as recursive functions, but recursive functions terminate in a different way. `for` loops will naturally terminate at the end of a sequence, but recursive functions could potentially carry on indefinitely unless a specified end condition is reached. It's important that the recursive function has a "base case" specified. The base case is the case for which recursion will end.

Let's look at how you can create a recursive function in Python. Assume that we need a function to list out the factorials of a given number. The factorial of a given number is the product of all numbers less than or equal to that given number. For example, the factorial of 3 is 3 * 2 * 1. This is a relatively simple calculation to carry out, but before we create a recursive implementation of a factorial function, let's create an iterative version of the function to see the steps we need to take.

If we were creating an iterative version of this algorithm, we would need to do the following:

- Create a variable that we'll multiply by the next number in the sequence.
- Initialize this variable to one.
- Using a range function and `for` loop, run from the value 2 (1 because of the 0-index base) to the target number plus one.
- For every index in the range, multiply the variable by the current sequence index, and then move to the next item in the range.

An iterative version of a factorial function would look something like this:

```
def factorial_calculation(num):
    current_value = 1

    for i in range(1, num + 1):
        current_value *= i

    return current_value

print(factorial_calculation(5))
```

When we use an iterative approach, we need to carry out the desired actions for every given element in our sequence. In contrast, when we create a recursive function, we can just specify the base case and what

105

the function should do until the base case is true. We then just continue to call the function until the base case is met.

A recursive version of the factorial calculation function might look something like this:

```
def recursive_calculation(num):
    if num != 1:
        return num * recursive_calculation(num - 1)
    else:
        return num

print(recursive_calculation(5))
```

Our base case/termination case is when the number to multiply has reached one. Otherwise, we take the input number and multiply it by one minus that number, and then the function calls itself. This would return a value of 120 when we run the program.

The concept of recursion can be somewhat confusing, but the more you work with recursive functions, the more you will come to understand them. It's advised that you spend some time trying to write recursive functions on your own.

11.2 - Lambda Functions

On occasion, you may find that you need a function to carry out a relatively simple task. In cases where writing an entire function seems unnecessary, you can use a Lambda function. Lambda functions are functions without names that still operate like regular functions. They are often used as quick, throwaway functions.

Lambda functions can take any number of arguments you'd like, but they will only contain a single expression, so you can only execute one piece of code with a lambda function. Note that lambda expressions return function objects.

Lambda functions are created just by using the `lambda` keyword. Here's the general format for creating a lambda expression:

```
lambda arguments: expression
```

Remember that you can only use a single expression when working with a lambda function. You also can't have any statements combined with the lambda operator. However, it's easy to return a value from the lambda function and assign it to a variable, which is accomplished just by using the assignment operator before the `lambda` keyword. The code below declares a lambda function that operates on an argument variable `num`, while the code after the colon is the logic of how the function should operate. It then assigns the value returned by the lambda function to a variable, which can then be passed to other functions as an argument.

```
multiplied_value = lambda num: num * 9
print(multiplied_value(3))
```

Lambda functions are primarily useful when you need a function that you will only use for a short time. One common use of lambda functions is when you need to endow a high-order function with a specific functionality because lambda functions can be used inside of regular functions. Lambda functions can also be used alongside other Python built-in functions such as the `filter()` and `map()` functions.

11.3 - Advanced Dictionary Handling: Min, Max, and Sort

As you work with dictionaries, you may find that you need to retrieve certain keys or values according to their ranking within the dictionary or that you need to sort the dictionary. Since there are no quick functions you can use to accomplish these tasks, we'll spend a little time here covering how to get the minimum/maximum dictionary entries, as well as how to sort a dictionary. Let's create a dictionary first.

```
ex_dict = {"key1": 31, "key2" : 29, "key3" : 45,
"key4": 97, "key5": 72}
```

In order to get the minimum and maximum values, we'd have to cast the keys and values as lists. We can do this with the `zip()` function. Remember that the order you pass in your arguments matters with this function, as it affects which list will be sorted first. The following code will turn the keys and values into lists and save them in variables.

```
min = min(zip(ex_dict.values(), ex_dict.keys()))
max = max(zip(ex_dict.values(), ex_dict.keys()))
```

We also call the `min()` or `max()` functions on these sorted lists and get the proper values.

```
print(min)
print(max)
```

Sorting a dictionary would work very similarly; you just have to call the `sorted()` function on the two lists. You could then print out the sorted lists next to one another to see the entire sorted dictionary.

```
print(sorted(vals), sorted(keys))
```

11.4 - Threading

Threading is the idea of running multiple processes alongside one another. While the code is not executed at the exact time, it divides the processes so that they run on different processors. One thread runs one process, while another thread is responsible for a different process. Threading can potentially enhance the speed at which a program executes, but it won't work in all cases. A significant advantage of using threads is that, as you begin to build more complex, large-scale programs, separating processes into different threads can provide extra clarity and focus to the design of a program.

To see how threading works, let's first write a basic program that allows us to carry out a certain number of actions while tracking how long those actions take to execute. We can use the built-in time module and the `perf_counter()` function to track how long our program took to run. The first time we call `perf_counter()`, it will start logging the execution time, and the second time we call `perf_counter()`, it will stop.

```
from time import perf_counter, sleep
list_1 = ['microphone', 'cup', 'TV', 'wallet', 'hat']
start = perf_counter()

def print_function():
    sleep(1)
    for i in list_1:
        print("Value:  " + i)
    print()

print_function()

end = perf_counter()
```

```
print('Time to finish: {} seconds '.format(round(end-
start, 2)))
```

The time needed to run this program should be about 5 seconds.

What if we had a second list and wanted to print it out in the same manner? You might assume it would double our run time. However, not necessarily. We can make use of extra resources the computer isn't using to create another thread and run the second function call in less time. We should see a benefit in processing time whenever a task is I/O bound, or just waiting on input and output to finish. During an I/O task, the computer is often just waiting to receive an input and not actually using a lot of computational resources. Threading allows us to have the computer continue working on other operations while waiting for I/O tasks to finish. Let's set up two threads to see this in action.

We can create a thread by using the `Thread()` function from the threading module. We then pass in the desired function as the thread by specifying the target. The syntax should look something like this:

```
import threading
thread_1 = threading.Thread(target=desired_function)
```

After you save instances of threads as variables, you need to use the `start` function on the variable:

```
thread_1.start()
```

We will need to make sure that the methods complete before we calculate the run-time. We can do this by using the `join()` function.

```
thread_1.join()
```

Now we can update the code above to create multiple threads and see how long the code takes to execute. Let's create a `for` loop to run the code we've created multiple times.

```python
from time import perf_counter, sleep
import threading

list_1 = ['microphone', 'cup', 'TV', 'wallet', 'hat']

start = perf_counter()

def print_function():
    sleep(1)
    for i in list_1:
        print("Value:  " + i)
    print()

t1 = threading.Thread(target=print_function)
t2 = threading.Thread(target=print_function)
t3 = threading.Thread(target=print_function)
t4 = threading.Thread(target=print_function)

t1.start()
t2.start()
t3.start()
t4.start()

t1.join()
t2.join()
t3.join()
t4.join()

end = perf_counter()
```

```
print('Time to finish: {} seconds'.format(round(end-
start, 2)))
```

If we run this program, we would see that it only takes about one second to run. That's because the computer input and output operations take very little time, and while the program is waiting on the sleep time, it can carry out the printing in the other threads.

Threading won't work to boost the speed of CPU-bound tasks. Therefore, tasks where data is being computed may take longer to complete if it is threaded.

11.5 - Packages and the Pip Package Manager

One of the best parts of Python is that it allows you to both easily and efficiently install and use code written by other people in your own Python projects. The Python community has created many useful and powerful functions and tools for other developers to use. Can you imagine if you had to write out every function you wanted to use by yourself? Building complex projects would take you forever if this were the case. Thankfully, there's an easy way to install modules and libraries (scripts and collections of scripts that other people have written) in Python through the Pip package manager.

If you have installed Python from a source package, such as the official Python website, you should have access to Pip immediately. You can confirm this by opening the command line and running the following command:

```
pip --version
```

If Pip is already present on your system, it will give you the version number as well as its install location. If Pip isn't installed on your system, you'll need to install it first. Look up the installation instructions for your specific OS and Python version. We'll be working with Pip to install some modules and work on some sample projects later in this book, so be sure you have Pip installed properly.

When you want to install a Python library or module with Pip, just open the command line and write the syntax as follows:

```
pip install ItemToInstall
```

You can also install a specific version by using the equals operator and specifying the desired version.

```
pip install ItemToInstall==1.5
```

Typing `pip help` will give you all the options and commands you can use and `pip search SearchTerm` will allow you to search for a specific package you'd like to install and give you a brief description of the package. `pip list` will provide you with a list of all the installed packages.

Let's say, for example, that you are working on a project and you need to tell other people what packages they will need to install. You can do this by using the command `pip freeze`. This will give you all the package names and version numbers in a single file. That means you can do the following to have pip generate a text file full of all your package names and versions:

```
pip freeze > requirements.txt
```

You can also download the requirements file of other people's projects and install the necessary files using pip. The syntax is as follows:

```
pip install -r requirements_file.txt
```

113

You can also check to see which packages are outdated by using `pip list --outdated`. You could then go through and update the outdated packages.

If you use pip regularly, the packages you install will be applied globally - throughout your entire system. However, what if you need greater control over what packages are installed? Let's say one project you are working on is compatible with one version of a library, but another project isn't. Installing the package globally would force you to choose between versions for your projects. Thankfully, there is a way to deal with this problem: we can set up a virtual environment to have increased control over which packages are utilized.

11.6 - Virtual Environments

Virtual environments allow you to separate your dependencies and packages into isolated, contained collections. As mentioned earlier, this is useful when creating projects that rely on specific versions of libraries or packages. With a virtual environment, you can install just the desired libraries and modules you want in the environment, and their presence won't impact any other environment you have on your computer.

The easiest way to set up virtual environments in Python is with a package called `virtualenv`. This can be installed to your global Python instance using the following command:

```
pip install virtualenv
```

It will be beneficial if you keep all your created environments in one place so that it'll be easier to find them. For this reason, it's suggested that you open your command line and create a new directory to place your environments in, using the `mkdir` command followed by the name of the directory you'd like to create. For example:

```
mkdir Environments
```

You'll then want to access that directory by using the `cd` command to change the current directory to the folder you just created:

```
cd Environments
```

We can now create a virtual environment by using the `virtualenv` command, followed by the name of the environment we want to create:

```
virtualenv test_environment
```

After you have created an environment, you need to activate avirtual environment to use it. We do this by changing the source Python environment with the `source` command. After the `source` command, we need to specify the source file we want to use, which is found within the `bin` folder of our environment, under `activate`. So, in this case, we would activate the environment like this:

```
source test_environment/bin/activate
```

We should now be in the environment that we have created. There should be an additional line included in the command prompt showing the current environment name, like this:

```
(test_environment)
```

If you do not see this, you can check to see which environment you are in by using the `which python` command in the command line. `which python` should return the path of the current Python environment. If you have successfully activated your virtual environment and you were to run `pip list`, you should see that the installed packages list is practically empty, except for perhaps a `setuptools` package. This makes sense, as the environment we've created has no packages included by default.

Let's try installing some packages to our new environment using pip. We'll install the requests, numpy, and PIL libraries.

```
pip install requests
pip install numpy
pip install PIL
```

If we ran `pip list` again, we'd see that the libraries/packages we installed are now included in the list of packages. Much like the global packages, we can save a list of the environment packages by using the `pip freeze` command.

```
pip freeze -local > requirements.txt
```

Finally, you can leave a virtual environment simply by typing `deactivate` and delete it by typing the following:

```
rm -rf test_environment
```

11.7 - Useful Libraries

Now that we understand what libraries are and how they can be installed, let's look at some of the most useful libraries that you may want to use in your projects. Most of these libraries can be easily installed with pip, although you'll want to check the documentation for these libraries to be certain. These libraries should also have a quick start guide on their site that you'll want to review. With that said, here are some of the most useful libraries for Python:

Requests - The Requests library allows you to easily create, customize, and execute HTTP calls, allowing you to get data from websites and work with it. It's the most popular HTTP library for Python and an important tool in any Python developer's toolkit.

Scrapy - Scrapy has been designed to make web scraping easier by more efficiently retrieving structured data from web pages. Scrapy allows you to create web-scraping bots (spiders) that you can easily extend and use in other programs.

SQLAlchemy - This is a toolkit designed to help users create, manage, and access SQL databases. SQLAlchemy is designed to allow flexible yet high-level database access integrated with the Python language. SQLAlchemy comes with a handy object-relational mapper (ORM) tool that lets users map object classes to database entries in multiple ways.

NLTK - The Natural Language Toolkit (NLTK) is a toolkit designed to provide Python developers with powerful natural language processing tools. NLTK allows the user to quickly carry out tasks like text classification, tagging, and parsing. It also contains many graphic illustration tools for text data.

Twisted - Twisted is a network application development tool that lets the user manage web servers, chat servers, mail servers, and more. Twisted is designed to be both flexible and secure, allowing developers to create servers and then scale small-footprint web servers up to larger high-traffic websites.

NumPy - NumPy is a library that helps developers manipulate data arrays and matrices, making the implementation of mathematical operations on large amounts of data much easier. NumPy comes with many functionalities that you can use out-of-the-box like linear algebra and transform functions.

SciPy - SciPy is an open-source python library containing functions used in technical and scientific computing. SciPy contains modules for tasks like statistics, linear algebra, and optimization. SciPy can also work with NumPy arrays.

Matplotlib - Matplotlib is a data visualization and graphing tool that is designed to create graphs and plots that look professional and high-quality. You can build multiple plots at once with the tool and control the look and layout of the plots. Matplotlib is also compatible with other data visualization tools like seaborn and ggplot.

Pillow - Pillow is an image manipulation library adapted from PIL (Python Imaging Library). Pillow improves upon PIL's many functions, updating them, and making them more user-friendly and intuitive. Pillow lets you open, manipulate, and save images. Pillow supports many different file formats and comes with a variety of image filters.

BeautifulSoup - BeautifulSoup is a library intended to make parsing HTML and XML documents as simple and intuitive as possible by allowing you to quickly extract the desired information from an HTML response. BeautifulSoup enables you to search, navigate, and even modify response trees, getting the information you need out of a document with ease.

wxPython - wxPython is a toolkit to create Graphical User Interfaces (GUI). wxPython lets the user design GUIs for use on a variety of different platforms, letting the user easily customize and manage GUI layouts and functions. It also functions across all major operating systems.

pyQT - pyQT is another GUI design toolkit. While pyQT may lack all the features that wxPython has, it's flexible in a way that wxPython often isn't by letting you rearrange, close, and restore panels during runtime. pyQT's widget elements and tools are also very clearly defined and intuitive to use.

Pygame - Pygame lets you design your own games in Python. Pygame gives the user tight, but intuitive control over game events and logic, though it's designed primarily for use in creating simple, 2D games.

Pyglet - Pyglet is a 3D game design and animation creation engine. Pyglet is capable of handling more complex instructions and animations than Pygame, allowing more low-level control.

Nose2 - Nose2 is a testing tool for Python that is designed to help developers test their functions and programs. While there are other testing options available, Nose2 is designed to make testing simpler to do and easier to grasp. Another testing framework is PyTest, which allows the user to write both small scale and large-scale functional tests.

Bokeh - Bokeh is a data visualization tool that supports the creation of interactive data visualizations. Bokeh utilizes both JavaScript and HTML to render graphics, providing this functionality in a convenient Python wrapper and allowing the graphics to be used in both dashboards and web applications. Bokeh allows the creation of multi-faceted statistical scenarios with simple keywords and functions.

Pandas - Pandas is one of the most used libraries in data science and data analysis. Pandas lets you easily manipulate data frames to select specific attributes of the data. Pandas can work with many different data formats, and it also comes with functions that help you handle missing data.

Scikit-learn - Scikit-learn is the go-to library for machine learning and data science. Scikit-learn makes it easy to transform and divide data into machine learning training and testing sets. It also comes with many different machine learning models and metrics. Scikit-learn can be used alongside other data science programs like NumPy and SciPy.

Keras - Keras is an excellent choice for those looking to start learning how to use deep neural networks and create complex machine learning models. Keras is an application programming interface (API) for the deep learning library Tensorflow and is intended to make creating and customizing deep neural networks as simple as possible.

11.8 - Working with Images

The following two chapters will be crash courses on how to work with the two most common types of data: images and text. We'll start by learning how to manipulate images in Python using the Pillow library. We will learn how to do things like display images, modify colors and sizes, as well as save the modified images.

To begin, we need to install the Pillow library. You'll need to check the install documentation on the Pillow site, as the installation instructions may vary depending on your OS. However, odds are you should be able to install it simply by running the following in the command line:

```
pip install Pillow
```

Now that we've installed Pillow, we can begin to use it. Just create a new Python file and import it with:

```
from PIL import Image
import os
```

You should choose an image file or two to work with. If you've placed the image files in the same directory as your Python file, you should be able to reference the images simply by providing the image name, but if not, you'll need to include the desired folder path containing your images. You can do this with:

```
sys.path.append('PathToFolder')
```

When we work with images, we create a variable that stores the image by using the assignment operator and the `Image.open()` function. Here's the syntax for creating an image object with Pillow:

```
image_obj = Image.open('image1.jpg')
```

Pillow comes with several different functions we can use on our image object. If we just wanted to show the image, all we would have to do is use the `show()` function:

```
image_obj.show()
```

The above code would display the image on the screen. The `show()` function enables us to quickly ensure we are working with the right image object.

What if we wanted to convert an image of one type to another? We could take our image object, clone it, and save it as another file type just by using the `save()` function. The `save()` function will create a new file with the specified file name and file type. That means if we wanted to make a new version of our image as a `png`, we could do this:

```
image_obj.save('image1.png')
```

Let's assume we needed to convert `jpg` images into `png` images, and the `jpg` images were all in one folder. We could do this using Pillow and the `os` module. All we would need to do is construct a `for` loop that selects all the files in the provided directory (or use a period by itself for the current directory), and then specify that if the file is a `jpg`, we want to open the file and save it as `png`. We would need to isolate the file name and the file type extensions from each other, as when we use the `save()`

function, we need to pass in the file name for each file in the `for` loop. Here's how this can be done:

```
for file in os.listdir('.'):
    # If the file ends with .jpg, open the file,
split the file on extension (using splitext) to get
the file name
    # Then save as .png using file name
    if file.endswith('.jpg'):
        file = Image.open(file)
        file_name,          file_extension          =
os.path.splitext(file)
        file.save('{}.png'.format(file_name))
```

What if you have a group of large images and wanted to resize them so that they take up less space? Pillow lets us resize images using the `thumbnail()` function. The `thumbnail()` function takes in two arguments, the pixel values on the X and Y axes. Take note that these values should be in a similar proportion to the values of your original image if you want the aspect ratio to be preserved. We could easily create a new, rescaled version of our image if we wanted by setting a size variable (so that we just need to change the variable if we want a different size) and then passing the variable into the `thumbnail()` function.

```
size_params = (400, 400)
image_obj.thumbnail(size_params)
image_obj.save('image1.png')
```

Let's briefly look at some of the other functions we could use to manipulate our images:

`rotate()` - The rotate function accepts the degree of rotation as its parameter and rotates the image by that many degrees. For example, the command `image_obj.rotate(90)` would rotate the image by 90 degrees.

`convert()` - The convert function accepts a mode argument that specifies how you want to convert the image. For example, `L` for converting to black and white and `RGB` for converting to an RGB scheme.

`filter()` - The filter function takes the type of filter you want to apply to your image. The filters available to use with Pillow can be accessed by importing the `ImageFilter` module. Afterward, you could pass in options like `blur`, `edge_enhance`, `contour`, or `sharpen`.

Pillow has many other useful functions and tools, check the official Pillow documentation (https://pillow.readthedocs.io/en/stable/) to learn more about what you can do with the library.

11.9 - Working with Text: Regular Expressions

We've previously discussed how to work with text in Python, but we'll now look at a more advanced text manipulation concept: regular expressions. Regular expressions allow you to search for and match specific strings and characters. Regular expressions are not unique to Python and much of what you'll learn here will carry over to other programming languages should you choose to learn them. However, Python does have a built-in regular expression module, the `re` module.

When working with regular expressions, you'll want to prefix your strings with the raw string formatter (r), which tells Python not to format the string in any way. This allows regular expressions to be able to work with the entire string. We saw this in an earlier chapter focused on working with text.

When creating a string you intend to use regular expressions on, set it up with the `compile` method that `re` provides, which will allow you to save your regular expression search patterns into a variable and make it simpler to reuse the desired pattern. Here's how we can create a regular expression (henceforth referred to as "regex") and use it to search a body of text.

```
import re

search_pattern = re.compile(r'you')

target_text = "Learning Python can be challenging, but
the more you practice the better you'll get. Look at
how far you've come already. You used to know nothing,
but now you know a lot in comparison. While there's
still so much more for you to learn, you can do it if
you persevere. --- 1 2 3 4 5 6 7 8 9 10. 123-456-7890.
Here's the thing we want to SEARCH."

# The finditer method
matched_text = search_pattern.finditer(target_text)
for m in matched_text:
    print(m)
```

If we ran this program, here's what we'd get (a printout of all the locations where our search pattern was found in the target text):

```
<_sre.SRE_Match object; span=(49, 52), match='you'>
<_sre.SRE_Match object; span=(73, 76), match='you'>
<_sre.SRE_Match object; span=(101, 104), match='you'>
<_sre.SRE_Match object; span=(156, 159), match='you'>
<_sre.SRE_Match object; span=(223, 226), match='you'>
<_sre.SRE_Match object; span=(237, 240), match='you'>
<_sre.SRE_Match object; span=(254, 257), match='you'>
```

If we ran a search for a capitalized you (YOU) instead, nothing would have been returned because regex search patterns are case sensitive. If we were trying to capture the periods in the target text and tried to use a search pattern like `re.compile(r'. ')`, it wouldn't work as we expect it to work. This is because the dot/period is a unique, reserved character in regex that codes for a specific type of character. If we did a search like that, it would return a match for almost everything. If we wanted to search for a period, we would need to escape the search pattern using an escape character like this:

```
re.compile(r'\.')
```

As mentioned, the dot/period is a special character in regex that you can use to retrieve any characters or words that match the criteria specified by the dot. The dot is used to tell the regex module that you want to search for "any character, except newline characters." Regex has many of these special search characters, including a character to retrieve digits in a string, which is the d character. This means that if we updated our search pattern, we should get back just the position of the digits that were in our target text. Let's update our search pattern and see what we get back when we run the program:

```
search_pattern = re.compile(r'\d')
```

If we ran the program with the search, we'd get back just the numbers:

```
<_sre.SRE_Match object; span=(273, 274), match='1'>
<_sre.SRE_Match object; span=(275, 276), match='2'>
<_sre.SRE_Match object; span=(277, 278), match='3'>
<_sre.SRE_Match object; span=(279, 280), match='4'>
...
...
```

It's possible to chain searches together in a single search pattern. If we wanted to search our string for the occurrence of three numbers in a row, we can just add three \d to our compile method.

```
search_pattern1 = re.compile(r'\d\d\d')
```

If we ran our search now, we'd get a match for the "123" in our target text.
```
<_sre.SRE_Match object; span=(295, 298), match='123'>
```

You can see how you would be able to specify a pattern that can match a phone number in a document, by chaining together \d characters and dashes.

```
search_pattern2       =       re.compile(r'\d\d\d-\d\d\d-
\d\d\d\d')
```

And here's the result:

```
<_sre.SRE_Match  object;  span=(295,  307),  match='123-
456-7890'>
```
You can accomplish this more elegantly by using a regex quantifier. Regex quantifiers allow you to choose how many characters you'd like to match for a certain search term. We can use either a single number in brackets or multiple numbers in brackets (the minimum and maximum we want to match). An equivalent to the above search term would be this:

```
search_pattern3 = re.compile(r'\d{3}-\d{3}-\d{4}')
```

If there are multiple possible characters in your desired return value, other quantifiers let you match with OR conditions. The asterisk (*) will match 0 or more characters, the plus (+) will match 1 or more characters, and the question mark (?) will match 0 or 1 character. This means you can find a single capital letter or multiple capital letters in our target text, followed by more capital letters using the + character.

```
search_pattern4 = re.compile(r'[A-Z]+[A-Z]{0,4}')
```

Running this search would get us:

```
<_sre.SRE_Match object; span=(0, 1), match='L'>
<_sre.SRE_Match object; span=(9, 10), match='P'>
<_sre.SRE_Match object; span=(85, 86), match='L'>
<_sre.SRE_Match object; span=(122, 123), match='Y'>
<_sre.SRE_Match object; span=(186, 187), match='W'>
<_sre.SRE_Match object; span=(309, 310), match='H'>
<_sre.SRE_Match object; span=(337, 343),
match='SEARCH'>
```

You can see it has matched both individual capital letters and multiple capital letters in sequence.

It's possible to search for a range of characters while using regular expressions by putting your search terms in brackets. You can either specify multiple characters you'd like to match (like this: [.',]) or look for a range of characters by using a dash (like this: [a - z]).
Note that when you search for a set of characters with brackets, the characters don't need to be escaped. If we wanted to search for all capital letters in our search text, we can do this:

```
search_pattern5 = re.compile(r'[A-Z]')
```

Running that search would get us:

```
<_sre.SRE_Match object; span=(0, 1), match='L'>
<_sre.SRE_Match object; span=(9, 10), match='P'>
<_sre.SRE_Match object; span=(85, 86), match='L'>
```

When searching for sets, you can use the ^ character to specify that you'd like to return everything that *isn't* part of the specified set.

There are more regex search formatting options as well. It's highly recommended that you spend some time playing around with regex to get used to it if you anticipate working with text a lot in your code. For completeness, here is a quick list of the different regex search characters and what they match, as well as the quantifiers:

"." matches any character except a newline character.

"\d" matches any digits in the string.

"\D" matches anything that's *not* a digit.

"\s" matches spaces, new lines, and tabs (all whitespace).

"\S" matches anything that's *not* spaces, new lines, or tabs (non-whitespace).

"\w" matches any word characters, alphanumerical characters.

"\W" matches any *non-word, non-alphanumerical* characters.

"^" matches the start of a string.

"$" matches the end of a string.

"\b" matches the boundary (beginning/end) of a word.

"\B" matches *non-word* boundaries.

"[]" matches the characters within the brackets.

"[^]" matches any characters that *aren't* within the brackets.

"*" matches zero or more characters.

"+" matches one or more characters.

"?" matches zero or one character.

"{}" matches the exact provided number of characters.

"{x, y}" matches a range of numbers, where x is the minimum value and y is the maximum value.

11.10 - SQLite

SQL is a query language used to manage relational databases. The following section will assume that you know SQL, but if not, feel free to skip it for now and come back when you have some experience with SQL.

Standard Python installers come with a built-in library intended to facilitate the creation, management, and integration of SQL databases in Python. This package is called SQLite, and we'll quickly cover how to create databases and tables, insert data, read data, and update data with SQLite. With SQLite, your entire database is a single file and there's no need to set up users or permissions to use it. Since Python comes with SQLite by default, we only need to import it.

When we want to interact with SQLite in Python, the first thing we need to do is establish a connection. The `connect()` function takes in the name of the database we want to connect to. If the database doesn't exist yet, one will be created. Here's how we'd create a database called `database1`.

```
import sqlite3
connection = sqlite3.connect("database1.db")
```

After we set up the database, we need to create an instance of a cursor, which is what will interact with the database.
```
c = connection.cursor()
```

We'll use the cursor to create a table in our database. Let's try creating a table that has different categories. We can create a table with the desired categories by calling the cursor's `execute()` function with the table name and the desire categories we want.

```
c.execute("CREATE TABLE IF NOT EXISTS table1(hats, shirts, pants, shoes, glasses)")
```

129

You don't need to capitalize SQL commands (SQL is completely blind to casing). Still, it is suggested that you follow the convention of capitalizing anything that is purely SQL, as it will help you distinguish what your statement does when you read it later.

To add data to a database, you can use the INSERT command in SQL along with the `execute()` function. The values you want to insert into the table need to be in the order you defined when you created the table.

```
c.execute("INSERT    INTO    table1    VALUES('Baseball',
'Henley', 'Khakis', 'Sneakers', 'Sunglasses')")
```
The other way to insert values into a table is to define them as variables and then pass the variables into the `execute()` function. This means you can easily combine your Python code with SQL statements. This is a dynamic form of data entry into SQL. When you use this form of entry, you need to specify the categories you want to insert the values into, followed by placeholder values, and then the variables. When we set the placeholders for the fields we want to enter the variables into, we pass them in as question marks. In other words, dynamic data entry into an SQL database looks like this:

```
c.execute("INSERT    INTO    table1    (hats,    shirts,    pants,
shoes,  glasses)  VALUES(?,  ?,  ?,  ?,  ?)",  (var1,  var2,
var3,  var4,  var5)
```

Whenever you have modified a table in some way, you need to save the changes you made. This is done by using the `commit()` function.

```
connection.commit()
```

In order to retrieve data we have entered into a SQL database, we also use the `execute()` function, and we need to select the data we want to extract from the desired table. After we select the data, we'll want to create a variable to hold it using the `fetch()` or `fetchall()` functions. `fetch()` gets a single row, while `fetchall()` gets everything that matches your query. Here's how we would get all the data we've entered.

```
c.execute('SELECT * FROM table1')
fetched_data = c.fetchall()
```

If you wanted to get more specific with your queries, you can apply regular SQL selection keywords to your query, such as WHERE and AND.

```
c.execute("SELECT * FROM table1 WHERE value='TargetValue' AND keyword='TargetKeyword'")
fetched_data = c.fetchall()
```

You may have realized by now that to interact with SQL through Python using the SQLite library, you just need to type in the SQL command you want, then execute the command. Here's how we can update and delete values:

```
c.execute("UPDATE table1 SET value = 'NewValue' WHERE value = 'OldValue'")
c.execute("DELETE FROM table1 WHERE value = 'ValueToDelete'")
```

After you've finished making changes, close both the cursor and connection to save memory.

```
c.close()
connection.close()
```

11.11 - JSON Data

As you write your own programs, you'll likely need to parse JSON (JavaScript Object Notation) data. The JSON data format is a data-interchange format that is intended to be easy for both humans and computers to interact with. Even though the JSON format is based on JavaScript language, it can be parsed by other programming languages like Python. JSON data is set up similarly to a Python dictionary, arranged in key/value pairs.

The key/value pairs in JSON data can be cast in multiple ways like an object, dictionary, keyed list, hash table, or associative array. The JSON data is also an ordered list and can be cast as a list, sequence, or array.

There are multiple libraries or packages that make handling JSON data with Python intuitive, including the Python built-in JSON package. Let's import the module:

```
import json
```

Python stores JSON data as a string. Let's create a simple JSON object that we can work with. We can parse a JSON string by using the `json.loads()` function. Below we'll create a JSON string named sample_json, and then turn it into a dictionary with the `json.loads()` function.

```
sample_json = '{"Name": "Jenna", "Friends": ["Laura",
"Dave"]}'
samples_dict = json.loads(sample_json)
```

Now let's try printing out the "Friends" portion of our dictionary. We do this by selecting the desired elements using bracket notation.

```
print(samples_dict['Friends'])
```

While we can create and parse JSON directly within Python, we can also load a JSON file directly into Python by using the `open()` function in conjunction with the `json.load()` function. For example, if we wanted to open up a file called `json_file.json`, here's how we can do that:

```
with open('file_path/json_file.json') as f:
    data_object = json.load(f)
```

If you want to turn a dictionary into a JSON, you can do that by using the `json.dumps()` function. Let's set up a dictionary that we'll use alongside the `dumps()` function:

```
computer_dict = {'Drink:': 'Coffee, Juice', 'Price':
'$3.00, $4.00', 'Container': 'Bottle, Mug'}
computer_json = json.dumps(computer_dict)
print(computer_json)
```

What if we wanted to create a JSON file with the dictionary we created? This can be done rather easily with the `json.dump()` function. (Please note this is distinct from `.dumps()`, be aware of the difference in the plural vs. singular form.) We'd just need to pass in the name of the dictionary we want to write to the file and the name of the file that we're trying to write to. For example, here's how we'd open a text file and write our dictionary to it:

```
computer_dict = {'Drink:': 'Coffee, Juice', 'Price':
'$3.00, $4.00', 'Container': 'Bottle, Mug'}
```

```
with open('computer.txt', 'w') as json_file:
    json.dump(computer_dict, json_file)
```

By doing this, we open a file called "computer.txt" using 'w' mode. Opening the file in "w" mode means that if the file hasn't been created already, it will be created for us. The `json.dump()` function takes the dictionary we created and makes it a JSON string, which is then written to the file we have specified.

We'll now look at how JSON files can be loaded and read. Let's take the JSON file we created above and load it into an object:

```
with open('computer.txt', 'r') as j:
    loaded_data = json.load(j)
    print(loaded_data)
```

If you want to select single elements from the object, just use bracket notation as shown above. You may have noticed that we used different functions of the json module depending on what we wanted to do with the JSON data. `json.dump()` is used when we wanted to dump a JSON object directly into a file, while `json.dumps()` is used when we needed the data as a string to print or parse it.

11.12 - Sys Module

One of the standard modules that is packaged with Python is the `sys` module. The `sys` module allows us to retrieve system-level information about the Python interpreter, print text out directly to the system, and accept arguments from the command line.

Let's see one of the ways we can interact with the interpreter by using the `stderr.write()` function. This function is used to write error text to the interpreter. If you write something within the function and run it, you'll see that the result is displayed in red error text. After you write the error statement, you'll probably want to use the following command:

```
stderr.flush().
```

Typically, Python buffers its outputs. However, using the `flush()` function ensures that everything is written to the terminal even though Python would normally wait and carry out other operations before writing out to the terminal. When dealing with errors, we will definitely want to ensure the error is written to the terminal.

```
import sys

sys.stderr.write('This is a sample error.')
sys.stderr.flush()
```

Now let's see how we can write standard, non-error messages directly to the terminal. We can do this with the `stdout.write()` function:

```
sys.stdout.write("This is regular text being delivered
directly to the terminal.")
```

The most useful function in the sys module is probably `sys.argv`. `sys.argv` enables you to pass arguments to your Python program using the command line, which opens the possibilities of using other programming languages to pass arguments to your Python program or interacting with the file yourself through the command line.

If you are going to pass arguments through the command line, you'd want to check to make sure there's more than one argument coming into the file. When running the file from the command line, the first argument will always be the name of the file, so we'd want to ensure that more than one argument is being passed. The following code will print out the second argument that comes in from the command line, assuming there is more than one argument:

```
if len(sys.argv) > 1:
    print(sys.argv[1])
```

Try opening the command line, navigating to the directory that holds your script, and running the file with a second argument coming after the file name. Your prompt should look something like this:

```
python file_name.py "Print This Text"
```

If we wanted to manipulate the arguments, we could do that as well:

```
if len(sys.argv) > 1:
    print(float(sys.argv[1]) + 10)
```

You could easily create a function to handle manipulation of the data as well. You would create a function that manipulates a value in some way and have the function take in a generic argument. Then you'd pass `sys.argv[1]` into the function call.

11.13 - Iterators vs Generators

In Python, iterators allow you to traverse through objects like lists. Iterators store information about the size and state of the object, tracking the items and indexes. Iterators allow you to move through a collection of elements one by one, but they aren't the only way you can accomplish this. You can also move through a series of elements using a generator. Let's take a quick look at the differences between generators and iterators.

The most basic type of iteration in Python is the `for` loop. It allows the user to loop through the values in a list and manipulate them in some fashion. For instance, here's a `for` loop that just prints out 1 through 4:

```
for x in [1, 2, 3, 4]:
    print(x)
```

There's an alternate way of iterating through an iterable object such as a list. You can create an instance of an iterator by using the built-in `iter()` function. This `iter()` function takes in iterables and creates an instance of a pre-defined `iter` class, which has the __next__ method. Invoking the __next__ method will return the next item in the list of iterables. The block of code below uses the `iter()` function to create an iterator instance and then invokes the __next__ method multiple times in order to print out 6, 7, 8:

```
y = iter([6, 7, 8, 9])
print(y.__next__())
print(y.__next__())
print(y.__next__())
```

Another example of an iterator is the built-in `range()` function, which takes up to three arguments and produces a list of numerical values within the specified range. All of Python's iterators are classes, and we can look at the code that drives them to better understand how they operate. The code below creates an iterator that behaves very similarly to the `range` class.

```
class range_ex:

# Initializes two elements - i (current item) and num
(number for range)
    def __init__(self, num):
        self.i = 0
        self.num = num

# returns self (returning self is what makes the
object iterable)
    def __iter__(self):
        return self
```

```
# when called, increment i and return as long as i is
less than the ending number
# otherwise stop iterating
    def __next__(self):
        if self.i < self.num:
            i = self.i
            self.i += 1
            return i
        else:
            raise StopIteration()
```

Notice that this is a complex process. To create an iterator, we need to create a class with two methods, monitor the internal state, and set a `StopIteration` condition. A generator in Python allows us to simply and elegantly yield elements sequentially, writing straightforward code that can be save memory.

Generators share a lot in common with iterators in that they both produce objects we can iterate through one value at a time. However, constructing a generator from scratch is typically simpler than creating an iterator from scratch. Generators use a set of rules defined by a function to create values, neglecting the need to store information about the internal state of an iterator, which saves on memory.

Generators are created by using a function along with the `yield` statement (instead of the `return` statement). When creating an iterator, methods such as `__iter__` and `__next__` are handled by Python automatically. Similarly, there's no need to call `StopIteration` because the generator just ceases producing values when a terminating condition is fulfilled.

Let's look at an example of how we can create a generator. The following code creates a generator that generates numbers, similar to the `range()` function, and it accepts a beginning value and an end value.

138

```
def gen_num(start, end):
    while start <= end:
        yield start
                start += 1

num_list = [ ]

for i in gen_num(5, 12):
    num_list.append(i)

print(num_list)
```

Here's what is printed back:

```
[5, 6, 7, 8, 9, 10, 11, 12]
```

The code above is an example of a generator function, but it's also possible to create a generator expression. Generator expressions are carried out like list comprehension. They can be used in situations where you need to quickly generate values, but writing a full generation function isn't necessary. For example, the following code would take every value in the range 1 to 5 and add it to itself. If we print the type of object, we will see that it is considered a generator object.

```
added = (i + i for i in range(1, 5))
print(type(added))
```

```
<class 'generator'>
```

In general, generators require less code to create and are more CPU and memory efficient. When working with small amounts of data, the difference in processing time and memory usage may not be significant, but if you are working with large volumes of data, then you'll want to use a generator.

11.14 - if __name__ == '__main__'

Let's discuss a line of code that can seem quite cryptic to those just starting to learn Python programming:

```
if __name__ == '__main__':
```

This line of code checks to see whether the source file for a module is in the main program running. If it is, then the code below this check will run. That's the short version of what this check does, but this line of code can be confusing for those relatively new to Python. For this reason, let's take a closer look at it.

Whenever a Python interpreter reads a file, two things happen. First, the interpreter sets the value of a special, hidden variable called `__name__`, and then it executes the code in the source file. This `__name__` variable is always present, and it's used to store the source of the module that is currently running. If you want, you can imagine that there's always a hidden `__name__` variable located at the top of your file, and the main script(as opposed to a secondary script you import modules from) will always have a value of `__main__` assigned to `__name__`. If a module isn't run directly, but is instead imported into another file and then ran, the `__name__` for that module is set to the name of the script that is importing the module.

Using the `if __name__ == '__main__'` check allows us to control how code is executed when the code is being ran directly vs. when a module is being imported. For example, try creating a new file called `module_1` and writing the following code in it:

```
if __name__ =='__main__':
    print("To be executed if ran directly.")
else:
    print("To be executed if imported.")
```

If you run this code directly from the script containing it, you'll get the following:

```
To be executed if ran directly.
```

You can then try opening a new script and importing the first file.

```
import module_1
```

If you then run the script, you'll get this printed out:

```
To be executed if imported.
```

You should use the `__name__` check if there's code that should only be executed when it's in the main file or if you have code that should only be executed when imported. You may not find yourself using the `if __name__ =='__main__':` check very often, but it's important to be aware that it exists because it lets you change the conditions of how your code is executed.

11.15 - Jupyter Notebooks

Jupyter Notebooks are versatile and robust tools that are useful in creating and presenting data science projects and other visual projects. Jupyter Notebooks allow you to write your code and share it with other people who can then run your code within the notebook and reproduce your results. Let's look at how Jupyter Notebooks can be created and used, starting with definitions of important terms.

A "notebook" is a unique document format that lets you combine code blocks, explanatory text, visualizations, and more into a single document. Due to the ease and convenience of creating presentations in a Jupyter Notebook, they are extremely popular for data science and analysis.

We can install the Jupyter notebook by using `pip`:

```
pip install Jupyter
```

After installing the Jupyter module, we can activate an instance of a Jupyter notebook by typing the following in the terminal:

```
jupyter notebook
```

This will launch an instance of a Jupyter notebook in your browser. The URL you will access the notebook control panel at is: `http://localhost:8888/tree`
Your notebook server should now be running and you'll be able to create a new Jupyter notebook by clicking "File" and then "New" in the drop-down list. When using a Jupyter notebook, you can give it a name by clicking on "Untitled" at the top of the page and typing in a name.

When working with a Jupyter Notebook, everything is contained in individual "cells," which you can add or delete. Cells can hold different types of media, like text, code, or images, but they need to be set to specific cell types depending on what you want to put in them. The cell type of your currently selected cell is always visible in the toolbar (when you first start a notebook, the toolbar should say "code"). You can change the cell type by opening the drop-down menu.

When you first create a Jupyter notebook, the type of the first cell is a code cell, so that you can write Python code in it. Let's try typing a print statement so we can confirm that our notebook is working properly:

```
print("We're writing in our Jupyter notebook!")
```

When you run a cell, the contents of the cell are executed. You can run a cell by clicking on the desired cell and then clicking the "Run" button or by using the keyboard shortcut Shift + Enter. Once your notebook has multiple cells in it, you can run them in any order you'd like by selecting the desired cell and running it. Note that things like variables and functions are only shared across your notebook if you run the cells in order (to have access to variable A, you must first run the cell where variable A is declared). You can also run all the cells from top to bottom by going up to the "Cell" option in the toolbar and selecting "Run All."

As you run the cells in your notebook, you may notice that there are numbers that appear in the brackets next to the cell. These numbers indicate which order the cells have been ran. For instance, the first cell that was ran will have a `[1]` next to it, while the second cell that was ran will show a `[2]` next to it.

In terms of the different cell types, there are four different kinds. The cell types in a Jupyter notebook are Code, Markdown, Raw NBConvert, and Heading.

The purpose of the code cells is obvious: to contain and run your code. The Markdown cells enable you to write and format text, and you can use them to add explanations to your code. Markdown syntax is based on HTML, but we won't cover Markdown formatting here. The key thing to remember is that you can style your explanatory text in several different ways like creating headings, creating lists, and altering text size. Jupyter Notebooks expect you to use Markdown to create headings, and for this reason, the Heading cell type is no longer supported in more recent versions of Jupyter Notebooks. Finally, the Raw NBConvert is for rare instances where you might need to convert a Notebook to another format and control the formatting during this conversion.

You can create new files with the file menu, and, under the options for saving files, you can even create a checkpoint that you can reload in case something goes wrong. This is accomplished by using the "Save and Checkpoint" option. The Edit menu allows you to copy, paste, cut, merge, and delete cells. The View menu lets you set the visibility of the toolbar and header. The Insert menu enables you to insert cells, while the Cell menu allows you to run a single cell, a group of cells, or all the cells within the notebook. The Kernel menu lets you restart your notebook, shut down the notebook kernel, or change which kernel is active. The Widgets menu is used to add and control JavaScript widgets, which can make your notebook more dynamic. Finally, the help menu contains relevant information on the Notebook's interface, shortcuts, and function.

11.16 - Unit Testing

As you create more complicated programs and begin to collaborate with other developers, testing your code to ensure that it functions appropriately will become extremely important. Unit Testing is a Python concept that refers to identifying and correcting bugs in the early stages of development before they become recurrent, hard to diagnose, and more expensive to patch.

"Unit tests" are tests used to evaluate the functionality of small blocks or "units" of code individually. The idea behind a unit test is that a module is being tested for proper functionality without referencing any other portions of code, meaning the units are self-contained when they are tested.

Unit testing is the core concept underlying Test-Driven Development. Test-Driven Development (TDD) begins with the programmer creating a Python unit test first, and then creating the code that will fulfill the conditions of the unit test. Two tools are required if you will be doing unit testing: stubs and mocks. "Stubs" contain descriptions of the interface of a module and they essentially stand in for dependencies/modules you use in Python. Meanwhile, a "mock" is a fake object which is used to assert how an object would be used in the natural execution of the code.
Python has a built-in testing module called `unittest`. Let's see how to use this library for unit-testing.

To begin, let's import the `unittest` module. We're also going to need a function to test, so let's use the function we created to calculate factorials back in the section about recursion.

```
import unittest

def factorial_calculation(num):
    current_value = 1
    for i in range(1, num + 1):
```

```
        current_value *= i

    return current_value
```

When we work with `unittest`, we need to create a class module that will hold the test cases. The class will inherit from the `TestCase` module in the `unittest` library. The class will also have a method in it that will test our function. When we create a testing method in a test class, it must start with `test_`. This way, the `unittest` module knows which methods are test methods. For us to run the test from within our IDE, we'll need to include the `if __name__ == "__main__":` check.

```
class Tester(unittest.TestCase):

    def test_factorial(self):
        result = factorial_calculation(5)
        self.assertEqual(result, 120)

if __name__ == "__main__":
    unittest.main()
```

The `assertEqual` method we've used here checks that the two provided values are equal. Under the "Classes and functions" section of Python `unittest` documentation, there's information on the various assert methods you can use.

If we run this test, here's what we'll get back:

```
Ran 1 test in 0.007s

OK
```

Here, we see that our single test ran and executed successfully; there were no errors that occurred when we ran the test. Note that "OK"

146

provided in the print statement simply means that no errors or warnings were found when the code ran. This can happen even when no tests ran. If your test method did not start with `test_`, as specified above, the method would be skipped, and you would get back an "OK" even though the number of tests ran was 0.

What would happen if we changed the arguments in the `assertEqual` method above to something that was incorrect? Let's change our test function to contain values that are incorrect:

```
class Tester(unittest.TestCase):

    def test_factorial(self):
        result = factorial_calculation(5)
        self.assertEqual(result, 100)
```

Now let's re-run the function and see what the output is.

```
Ran 1 test in 0.028s

FAILED (failures=1)
100 != 120

Expected :120
Actual   :100
```

This should be followed by a series of traceback text indicating the actual lines that caused the error. As you can see, our test method has caught an issue and displayed some information about the cause of the problem as well as the expected value that would satisfy the assert condition.

As you test your code, you'll want to try to test cases that could lead to an error. A common practice is to test your code with edge cases and both negative and positive numbers. Your goal is to write good tests that can help you track down potential cases where your code will fail. Let's explore this idea by testing a division function:

```
def divide_numbers(r, s):
    if s == 0:
        raise ValueError("Can't divide by zero.")
    result = r / s
    return result
```

In this case, we would want to construct a test that would look like this:

```
class TestDiv(unittest.TestCase):

    def test_divide(self):
        result = divide_numbers(-1, -1)
        self.assertEqual(result, 1)
```

We'd also want to test what happens if we divided -1 by 1, as well as similar cases. Note that it is possible to have an instance where your tests pass, but your code will still break in use. For example, let's say you were accidentally using the floor division operator in the division function instead of the regular division operator. Since floor division doesn't return a remainder, a potential issue would be missed if all your tests only looked for whole number returns. You would need to explicitly test a case where the expected return value is a float for the problem to be caught. This is why, as you test, you'll want to think of various scenarios that can cause breakages in your code.

What if you need to test that an error condition, such as a ValueError, is working properly? Evidently, you can't just write a statement that makes the error occur, or the test module will think something failed. To check if an exception handler is working, you'll want to use a context manager. You can use a context manager by using the `with` conditional and pass

148

in the error handler you want to use alongside `assertRaises` within your test method:

```
class TestDiv(unittest.TestCase):

    def test_divide(self):
        result = divide_numbers(-1, -1)
        self.assertEqual(result, 1)

        with self.assertRaises(ValueError):
            divide_numbers(5, 0)
```

If you need to create objects that must be referenced repeatedly during testing, like a class object stored in a variable, you can do this by using the `setUp` and `tearDown` methods. The `setUp` method will run itself before any of the test code is executed, meaning you can use it to create the object you need, which you can then reference with `self` throughout testing. The `setUp` method is constructed in the test class with the following syntax:

```
def setUp(self):
    self.variable_name                        =
Object_Class(object_arguments)
```

You may not find yourself using the `tearDown` method very frequently, but an instance where it might come in handy is when working with methods that create new files in a directory. In this case, your setUp method could be used to create the directory while the tearDown method would delete the created files.

Earlier, we mentioned the concept of mocks and mocking. Knowing how to use mocks would be important when testing a function that manipulates outside data. Consider a function that pulls information from an external database or website: you wouldn't want the test to evaluate your function as having failed if the external data source was having problems, but rather if the function itself had problems. We won't cover how to use mocks or stubs here, but you should be aware of their existence as you go on to test your code.

Chapter 12:
Projects

The final section of this book will involve completing two different projects. One project will be a simple project that only involves the manipulation of text. The second project is more complicated: it involves collecting data from a source on the internet and then displaying that data through a GUI (Graphical User Interface) on your computer. All the code necessary to complete the projects will be given. Still, much like the coding exercises earlier in the book, you are highly encouraged to try solving the problems yourself before looking at examples of how the projects can be completed.

12.1 - Project 1: Story Idea Generator

In this project, we'll be creating a story idea generator. We'll have a sentence template that we fill in with phrases to create an idea for a story. Our program will use lists of characters, objects, themes, etc. and select one item from the list at random. We'll then insert these random choices into the sentence template to create a story prompt.

Let's start by thinking about the steps we'd need to take to accomplish the project's goal. Our goal is to generate a story prompt/idea from several different, pre-defined attributes. For instance, we can have a list of characters and settings to choose from. This also means that we can start by creating a sentence template and choosing the fields we'd like to insert into the sentence. So, let's begin by setting up our sentence template. It can look something like this:

```
"In" + " " + setting + ", there is a" + " " +
protagonist + " " + "who" + " " + conflict +
antagonist + "."
```

You can see that we want to insert an item from four different categories into our template. Do you know how this can be accomplished with a single function? Try writing your own generation function before you look at how it can be created.

Here's one way we can write a generation program.

We'd want to start by creating four lists that will hold items belonging to these various categories. You can go with any theme or genre that you would like, but in this instance, we'll theme our categories around sci-fi concepts. We'll have the following categories: setting, protagonist, conflict, and antagonist. The "protagonist" field will be comprised of two separate categories: gender and occupation. To begin with, we'll create lists of possible items for all the categories.

```
setting = ["future Seattle", "future New York",
"future Tokyo", "a dystopia", "a virtual world", "a
base stationed on the moon", "a utopia", "a space
station", "a city under the sea", "an artificial
island", "an underground complex"]

gender = ["man ", "woman ", "robot ", "third gender ",
"animal ", "mutant "]

occupation = ["writer", "pilot", "detective",
"cyborg", "doctor", "soldier", "hacker", "engineer",
"corporate employee", "actor", "scientist", "racer",
"street rat", "delivery person"]

antagonist = ["a rogue AI", "a gigantic corporation",
"a secret society", "a collection of robots", "groups
of internet trolls", "a group of aliens", "a
devastating virus", "a corrupt government", "new
bandits", "new pirates", "a powerful street gang", "a
```

disruptive technology", "a clone of the hero",
"genetically-engineered monsters"]

```
conflict = ["tries to stop ", "falls in love with ",
"seeks revenge against ", "runs away from ", "fights
against ", "defends against ", "exceeds beyond ",
"explores with ", "attempts to befriend ", "is in
competition with ", "must infiltrate ", "tries to
redeem "]
```

Now that we've created lists for our different categories, we can randomly select an item from these lists and insert it into our sentence template. Fortunately, we can use the built-in library `random` and the `random.choice()` function to randomly select an item from our lists. Import the module and then wrap the lists in the `random.choice()` function, like this:

```
import random
setting = random.choice(
                ["future Seattle", "future New York",
"future Tokyo", "a dystopia", "a virtual world", "a
base stationed on the moon", "a utopia", "a space
station", "a city under the sea", "an artificial
island", "an underground complex"])
```

. . .

After wrapping the lists in the `random.choice()` function, we can pass in the variables into our template and print it out.

```
print("In" + " " + setting + ", there is a" + " " +
protagonist + " " + "who" + " " + conflict +
antagonist + ".")
```

That's all we needed to do to get our story generator working. Here's a sample of what it printed out:

```
"In   a  base   stationed   on   the   moon,   there   is   a   robot
cyborg who explores with a group of aliens."
```

However, what if we wanted to generate a bunch of story prompts instead of just one? If we just call the print statement a few more times, we'll find out that all the printed prompts are the same because Python preserves the random choice across all the print statements, not to mention that printing the statement multiple times is repeating ourselves unnecessarily. It would be much simpler if we wrapped the code in a function that took in the number of sentences we'd like to generate as an argument. See if you can figure out how to write a function that generates as many story prompts as the user specifies.

Once you've had a shot at composing the function, review the example below to see one way it can be accomplished.

To create a function that will print the desired number of story prompts and ensure that the story prompts are different, you would need to use a while loop and have the `random.choice()` calls inside of that while loop. You want to keep looping until the number of iterations is equal to the desired number of prompts, so you'll start by creating a variable to keep track of the number of prompts created and then increase that value before ending the current loop (but after printing the prompt). Given this, the entire function should look something like this:

```
def plot_gen(num_gen):

    i = 1

    while i <= num_gen:
            setting = random.choice(
```

```
                ["future Seattle", "future New York",
"future Tokyo", "a dystopia", "a virtual world", "a
base stationed on the moon", "a utopia",
                    "a space station", "a city under the
sea", "an artificial island", "an underground
complex"])
        ...

        ...

        ...

        print("In" + " " + setting + " ...)
        i += 1

plot_gen(5)
```

Congrats on creating your first Python program! Now we'll move onto the second program.

12.2 - Project 2: Weather Application

In this project, we'll be building a simple weather application. This weather application will gather weather data from an outside source and deliver it to the user through a simple Graphical User Interface (GUI). More specifically, we'll create a GUI that allows the program's user to request information about the weather in the desired city from an outside source.

If you don't want to bother with creating the GUI and just want to print the weather data straight to your terminal, you can. However, you won't improve your skills unless you challenge yourself. Learning how to create the GUI will take some initiative on your part, as you'll need to peruse the documentation of the library used to create the GUI. You should learn how to read library documentation effectively because you'll need it to use libraries in the future.

This project will be more complex than the first project and it will involve using several different libraries and modules. Because this project is more complex, let's break it down into smaller problems. We'll solve these minor problems and then use the building blocks we've created to make our larger app.

Let's take a moment to think about how we could go about creating a weather app. We know that we'll need to get the weather data from somewhere and we also know that once we've collected the data, we'll need to transform it into a format that our application can use. Finally, we know that once we've created functions to collect and transform the data, we'll need to construct a GUI that will let the user make requests and display the requested weather data. Essentially, we can break this problem down into three smaller ones:

- Creating a function to get the weather data
- Creating a function to transform the weather data into a format we can display
- (Optional) Creating a GUI that allows the user to launch the functions we have created and displays the result back to the user

Let's start by creating a function that will get the weather data from an outside source.

When it comes to extracting data from the web, there are multiple ways this can be done. You could build a web scraper that goes to a URL and extracts the desired HTML elements from the webpage. However, designing a web scraper from scratch can prove time-consuming, and there is usually an easier way of getting data. Many websites offer an Application Programming Interface (API), which is a method of interfacing with the website and its data in a simpler, more intuitive fashion. APIs frequently offer easy-to-use methods you can integrate with your code to get relevant data, greatly simplifying the process of data collection.

To collect the weather data, we're going to be using the website OpenWeatherMap and its API. You'll want to create a new account, which can be done by going to the API section of the website (https://openweathermap.org/api) and then selecting the "Sign Up" option. After you've created your account and signed into the website, you'll want to write down your API key. Get your API key by going to the "API Keys" tab from the home page after sign-in. The API key lets you make use of their API and it must be provided when you make calls to the website through your Python app. Be sure to write your key down and place it in your Python program as a variable as shown below:

```
api_key = "YOUR API KEY HERE"
```

OpenWeatherMap gives you access to a 5-day/3-hour forecast at the free subscription tier. After getting your API Key, subscribe to the free tier of the 5-day/3-hour forecast and get the link that you'll need to send API requests to. The link you'll need to send calls to is the following link:

https://api.openweathermap.org/data/2.5/weather/

Go ahead and save this URL as a variable as shown below:

```
url                                           =
"https://api.openweathermap.org/data/2.5/weather/"
```

By using these two variables as your starting point, can you figure out how to develop a function that will do the following:

- Take in a city to get weather data about
- Make a call to the URL
- Fetch the desired data (returned in the form of a dictionary)
- Format the data as a JSON

As a hint, know that you can do this with one of Python's built-in libraries (the "requests" library). When making the call to the API, three arguments are expected: your API key, the target city, and the units (imperial or metric) you want the weather data to be in.

Feel free to continue after you have given this a try.

We can get data from a URL by using the built-in requests module. We just need to import the module and then use the `get()` function. When using the `get()` function, we can pass in some optional parameters in the form of a dictionary. While not every request needs these parameters, this particular request does. We need to pass in the API key, the query city, and the units. We pass these arguments to `get()` in the form of a dictionary. The data we get back is returned in the form of a dictionary and we can make it into a JSON by using the `json()` function.

Your function to get the weather data should look something like this:

```
import requests

def get_data(city):
    api_key = "YOUR API KEY HERE"
    url =
"https://api.openweathermap.org/data/2.5/weather/"
    arguments = {"APPID": api_key, "q": city, "units":
"imperial"}
    data = requests.get(url, params=arguments).json()
```

That's the function to handle requesting the data. Now we need to select the desired elements from the response. Let's go ahead and print out the data variable to see what kind of elements are available for us to use. Let's provide a city for our function and then print out the response:

```
def get_data(city):
```

```
    api_key = "YOUR API KEY HERE"
    url =
"https://api.openweathermap.org/data/2.5/weather/"
    arguments = {"APPID": api_key, "q": city, "units":
"imperial"}
    data = requests.get(url, params=arguments).json()

    print(response_format(data))

get_data("Seattle")
```

When running this program, we get back a long string containing the entire response:

```
{'coord': {'lon': -122.33, 'lat': 47.61}, 'weather':
[{'id': 500, 'main': 'Rain', 'description': 'light
rain', 'icon': '10d'}], 'base': 'stations', 'main':
{'temp': 39.16, 'feels_like': 35.92, 'temp_min': 36,
'temp_max': 42.01, 'pressure': 1021, 'humidity': 93},
'visibility': 16093, 'wind': {'speed': 0.94, 'deg':
178}, 'rain': {'1h': 0.25}, 'clouds': {'all': 90},
'dt': 1579296427, 'sys': {'type': 1, 'id': 5451,
'country': 'US', 'sunrise': 1579276296, 'sunset':
1579308396}, 'timezone': -28800, 'id': 5809844,
'name': 'Seattle', 'cod': 200}
```

We don't want to use all of this information, so let's only select a few elements to use. We'll choose to just work with the city name, the weather description, the current temperature, wind, and "feels like."

We now want to extract just the data that's relevant to us from the response. We can do this by selecting individual elements from the JSON and saving them as variables. We should also insert a way to handle instances where the query city isn't recognized by OpenWeatherMap's

API. Try pulling only the relevant data out of the JSON and then joining these variables into a full string, while controlling for instances where the city isn't found.

After you've tried to solve the problem yourself, feel free to go on.

We can use `try` and `except` to handle instances where the queried city isn't found. Within the try condition (presuming success), we can select data from the JSON with bracket notation. Finally, we just join relevant items into a full string and use some string formatting. We can either write a second function to handle the parsing of JSON or just include this logic in our current function. In general, you want to try and separate tasks into different functions, but to keep things simple, we'll add the new code to our current function:

```python
def get_data(city):

    api_key = "YOUR API KEY HERE"
    url                                       =
"https://api.openweathermap.org/data/2.5/weather/"
    arguments = {"APPID": api_key, "q": city, "units":
"imperial"}
    data = requests.get(url, params=arguments).json()

    try:
        name = data['name']
        desc = data['weather'][0]['description']
        temp = data['main']['temp']
        wind = data['wind']['speed']
        feels_like = data['main']['feels_like']
        full_string = 'Location: {} \n Conditions: {}
\n' 'Temperature (F): {} \n' 'Wind (MPH): {} \n'
'Feels Like (F): {}'.format(name, desc, temp, wind,
feels_like)
```

```
except:
    full_string = "No matching location found. \n
Please check location and try again."
```

We now have the data we want. If we wanted to stop here, we could just print out `full_string` to the terminal and be done. Adding `print("full_string")` to the function and running it should give us a result like the following:

```
Location: Seattle
Conditions: light rain
Temperature (F): 39.52
Wind (MPH): 0.94
Feels Like (F): 36
```

We could stop there if we felt like it, but why not make something a little more visually impressive? We can create a GUI for our program, which will let users enter a city location and have the relevant data returned to them within the app instead of being printed to the terminal. This can be accomplished with another Python module: Tkinter. Tkinter is a library that helps you create GUIs for programs with a minimal amount of code and if you have installed the most recent version of Python, the library should be included by default. If you installed an older version of Python, you should check to see that Tkinter is installed and operational. You can check to see if Tkinter is working by importing the module and using the `test()` function.

```
import tkinter
tkinter._test()
```

If you don't have Tkinter operational on your machine, you should read through the installation instructions on the Tkinter website (https://tkdocs.com/tutorial/install.html) and install it before going further.

Here's what the app GUI we'll be creating looks like:

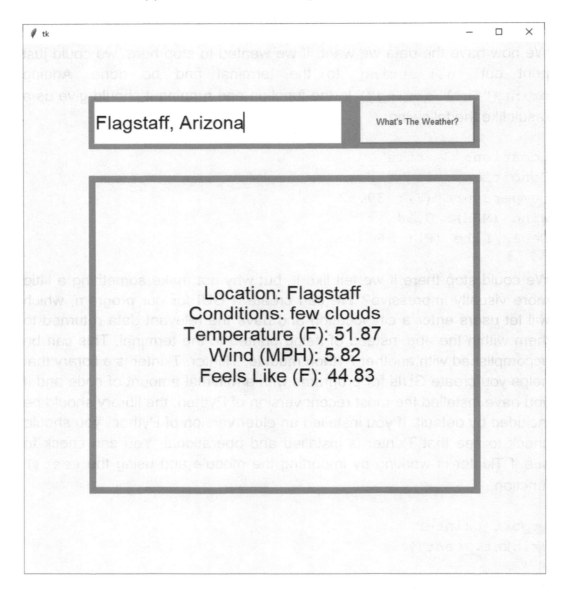

We won't go too deeply into the inner workings of Tkinter. Rather we'll just cover the basics here. As mentioned, you'll need to practice reading documentation and it's encouraged that you go to the documentation for

Tkinter (https://docs.python.org/3/library/tk.html) and learn how to make use of it. That said, let's go over the basics of how Tkinter operates.

Tkinter works by drawing frames, which can hold a variety of content such as images and text. To draw the frames, the root window must first be declared. The root window activates an instance of Tkinter that will hold the individual elements/the individual frames. You must also specify a canvas that the individual elements will be drawn on. After declaring the root window and the canvas to place items on, you can create a frame.

Let's start by importing Tkinter and creating a root object, which is accomplished by calling the `Tk()` function.

```
import tkinter as tk

root = tk.Tk()
```

Knowing that you need to first create an instance of the root Tkinter object and then create a canvas and frame on top of it, can you figure out how to create your first Tkinter frame and place it on the canvas? Once you have created a frame, place it in the upper quarter of your canvas. As a hint, look up the Tkinter documentation for the "Canvas" and "Frame" functions.

After trying to create a canvas and frame by yourself, you can review the example below to see how this is done.

The canvas is specified as a location within the root window. The canvas is created with the canvas function, which takes the root as an argument as well as a desired height and width in pixels. After the canvas object is created, you can manifest it in the root window with the `pack()` function. Once the root and canvas objects have been created and placed, a frame can be created with the `Frame()` function. The frame function allows you to pass in a background color (bg) and a border width (bd) in pixels. After the frame is created, you can place it where you'd like within the canvas by using the `place()` function and setting the `relx` and `rely` values. This can be done with the following code:

```
# Static height and width variables
w = 700
h = 800

# container is a location within the root window
canvas = tk.Canvas(root, height=h, width=w)
canvas.pack()

frame = tk.Frame(root, bg="#cc2929", bd=8)
frame.place(relx=0.5,      rely=0.1,      relwidth=0.75,
relheight=0.1, anchor="n")
```

Now that we've created one frame, let's try creating another frame. The second frame will go in the bottom three-quarters of our canvas. Can you figure out how to create a second frame after creating the first one?

It can be done like this:

```
frame_2 = tk.Frame(root, bg="#cc2929", bd=10)
frame_2.place(relx=0.5, rely=0.25, relwidth=0.75,
relheight=0.6, anchor="n")
```

Now that we've created the two frames, we can start creating the other features of the GUI. We'll need three things to complete our GUI: a text input field that allows users to enter the name of a city, a button that launches our `get_data` function using the given text as an input, and a label that we will populate with the text returned from the API call.

To create these elements of the GUI, we can use three Tkinter functions: `Entry`, `Label`, and `Button`. Check the documentation for these methods and see if you can determine how to add them to the GUI.

If you've given an attempt to create the three GUI elements, feel free to read on.

Creating the `Entry` and `Label` fields is easy enough because you just need to pass in the desired frame as the first argument and then optional information like font and font size. After this, the `place()` function is used to place the elements. The button is created by using the button function and passing in arguments like the target frame, the text, the font, and an additional argument - command. The command argument lets us tell Tkinter what function we want to run when the button is clicked and this is where we'll pass in the `get_data` function. We do need to pass in the argument using a lambda function and we want to `get()` what is currently in the `entry` field.

```
# Create and place interactive GUI items
entry = tk.Entry(frame, font=('Arial', 22))
entry.place(relwidth=0.65, relheight=1)

label = tk.Label(frame_2, font=('Arial', 22))
label.place(relwidth=1, relheight=1)

# use the lambda function to update values in tkinter
function calls
Button = tk.Button(frame, text="What's The Weather?",
fg='blue', font=('Arial', 10), command=lambda:
get_data(entry.get()))
button.place(relx=0.7, relwidth=0.3, relheight=1)
```

Back in our `get_data` function, we need to add the following line of code to the very bottom:

```
label['text'] = full_string
```

This assigns the text in the `full_string` variable to our label. This should be all we need to do to get our GUI functioning, except tell Tkinter to execute the main loop and render the items we want to draw. We can display our GUI by adding this bit of code:

```
root.mainloop()
```

You should now be able to run the program and type in a location you'd like the weather for. After hitting the "What's the Weather?" button, the relevant data should be displayed in the lower frame.

We're almost done, but can we add some extra functionality to make our app a bit more responsive? Currently, most of the app is gray. What if we wanted to include a background image in our app to give our users something to look at when the weather data is returned? We could do this by creating a label that will be filled in with an image and using it as the background of our app. Let's create a background image that will change depending on the type of weather data received. For example, display a rainy image when the weather data contains rain, and a snowy image when it contains snow.

To create this functionality within our app, we would first need to construct a label used for the background image within the main portion of our app (the Tkinter build instructions). After this background label is created, we want to create a function that checks to see if the description of the weather contains certain terms, like rain or snow. We'll then choose an image to represent these weather events and update the background image based on the received description data.

Let's start by creating our background image as a label. We can do this by using the `PhotoImage()` function from Tkinter. We can leave it blank for now since we'll update it in our function. We then make a Label out of the image object. Let's place the following code between the "canvas" and "frame" portions of the code that builds our Tkinter app.

```
background_image = tk.PhotoImage()
background_label                    =                    tk.Label(root,
image=background_image)
background_label.place(relwidth=1, relheight=1)
```

We'll now need to pick out some images to represent the different weather states we're interested in tracking (for this demonstration, we'll only use three: rainy, snowy, sunny). You can go to a free image website like Pixabay to search for images that match this criterion and use any images you'd like. Save them as a .jpg and save them into the same folder as your app. Now we'll need to create a function that checks to see if certain strings are in the description of the weather. If the strings are found, we'll update the background image to the image that matches the description.

Let's start with the function that will check the description for the presence of certain strings and assign an image to a variable if that string is found. The function will look for the presence of "rain" or "snow" in the description; otherwise, it will choose a sunny image.

```
def get_image_type(description):
    if "rain" in description:
        image_type = "rain.jpg"
    elif "snow" in description:
        image_type = "snow.jpg"
    else:
        image_type = "sunny.jpg"
    return image_type
```

Back in our get_data function, we should create an image_type variable that will hold the returned value from our function. While we do this, let's also choose a default image and set it as the default value for our image_type. That way, there's always a default image to fall back to, and an error won't occur. Go ahead and choose another image you'd like to use for the default image. We'll create the `image_type` variable near the top of the `get_data` function as shown below:

```
image_type = "default.jpg"
```

Now we must call our `get_image_type` function. We want it to take the description of the weather data JSON, which we've saved as a variable called `desc`. We need to put that under the `try` keyword so that the function has access to the `desc` variable. Put the following line of code just under the `full_string` variable within the `try` condition:

```
image_type = get_image_type(desc)
```

Now that we have the `image_type` specified and have allowed it to change depending on the weather data we receive, all we need to do is update the `background_label` variable. We'll do this within our `get_data` function so that the update occurs when we click the "What's the Weather?" button. We can update the image by creating a new image object, which is most easily done with the `Image.open()` and `ImageTk.PhotoImage()` functions from PIL. ImageTk is a special module built into PIL that is designed to work with Tkinter. First, let's import the modules we need.

```
from PIL import ImageTk, Image
```

Now we just need to create a new image object, which gets `image_type` as its argument. We then use the `.configure()` function on `background_label` and tell the function we want to configure the label to accept a new image. Finally, we update the label by setting the label's image property to the new image.

```
new_image = ImageTk.PhotoImage(Image.open(image_type))
background_label.configure(image=new_image)
```

```
background_label.image = new_image
```

Here's what our `get_data` function should look like now:

```
def get_data(city):

    api_key = "YOUR API KEY HERE"
    url                                          =
"https://api.openweathermap.org/data/2.5/weather/"
    arguments = {"APPID": api_key, "q": city, "units":
"imperial"}
    data = requests.get(url, params=arguments).json()
    image_type = 'default.jpg'

    try:

        name = data['name']
        desc = data['weather'][0]['description']
        temp = data['main']['temp']
        wind = data['wind']['speed']
        feels_like = data['main']['feels_like']
        full_string = 'Location: {} \n Conditions: {}
\n' 'Temperature (F): {} \n' 'Wind (MPH): {} \n'
'Feels Like (F): {}'.format(name, desc, temp, wind,
feels_like)
        image_type = get_image_type(desc)

    except:
        full_string = "No matching location found. \n
Please check location and try again."

    label['text'] = full_string
```

169

```
    new_image                                    =
ImageTk.PhotoImage(Image.open(image_type))
    background_label.configure(image=new_image)
    background_label.image = new_image
```

Now when our app gets weather data, it should look much more impressive.

That looks much better. We've also reached the end of the project. Feel free to try and add new features, customize the layout of the GUI, or try and optimize the code to your liking.

Congratulations on making it to the end of this project and on making it to the end of this book! You've come a very long way, and while there's still much to learn, you have the basics down, giving you the foundation to learn more advanced concepts and build complex projects. As you continue your Python journey, don't forget to practice often and keep your skills sharp. Good luck with all your future programming projects!

References

PyCharm: The Python IDE for Professional Developers by JetBrains. (n.d.). Retrieved December 2019, from https://www.jetbrains.com/pycharm/.

PEP 8 -- Style Guide for Python Code. Guido van Rossum, Barry Warsaw, Nick Coghlan (01-Aug-2013). Retrieved December 2019, from https://www.python.org/dev/peps/pep-0008/.

Chan, J. (2017). *Learn Python in one day and learn it well: Python for beginners with hands-on project*. North Charleston, SC: CreateSpace Independent Publishing Platform.

Python, 5. Data Structures. (n.d.). Retrieved December 2019, from https://docs.python.org/3/tutorial/datastructures.html.

GeeksForGeeks, DevanshuAgarwalCheck. (2018, February 7). Decision Making in Python (if, if..else, Nested if, if-elif). Retrieved December 2019, from https://www.geeksforgeeks.org/decision-making-python-else-nested-elif/.

GeeksForGeels, loops in python. (2017, June 7). Retrieved from https://www.geeksforgeeks.org/loops-in-python/.

DigitalOcean. (2019, August 29). Break, Continue, and Pass Statements in For and While Loops. Retrieved December 2019, from https://www.digitalocean.com/community/tutorials/how-to-use-break-continue-and-pass-statements-when-working-with-loops-in-python-3.

Python, Built-in Exceptions. (n.d.). Retrieved December 2019, from https://docs.python.org/3/library/exceptions.html.

GeeksForGeeks, Global, and Local Variables in Python. (2018, September 6). Retrieved December 2019, from https://www.geeksforgeeks.org/global-local-variables-python/.

Kinsley, H. (n.d.). Args and Kwargs - Intermediate Python Programming p.25. (2016, December 15) Retrieved December 2019, from https://www.youtube.com/watch?v=gZB_ENJD34E.

Python, Built-in Functions. (n.d.). Retrieved December 2019, from https://docs.python.org/3/library/functions.html.

Schafer, C. (2016, July). Python OOP Tutorial 3: classmethods and staticmethods. Retrieved December 2019, from https://www.youtube.com/watch?v=rq8cL2XMM5M.

Schafer, C. (2016, July). Python OOP Tutorial 4: Inheritance - Creating Subclasses. Retrieved December 2019, from https://www.youtube.com/watch?v=RSl87lqOXDE

Schafer, C. (2016, August). Python OOP Tutorial 5: Special (Magic/Dunder) Methods. Retrieved December 2019, from https://www.youtube.com/watch?v=3ohzBxoFHAY

Jabeen, H. (2018, April.). Reading and Writing Files in Python. Retrieved December 2019, from https://www.datacamp.com/community/tutorials/reading-writing-files-python.

Awasthi, A. (2018, June 28). Thinking Recursively in Python. Retrieved December 2019, from https://realpython.com/python-thinking-recursively/.

GeeksForGeeks, max() and min() in Python. (2019, November 29). Retrieved December 2019, from https://www.geeksforgeeks.org/max-min-python/

Schafer, C. (2019, September). Python Threading Tutorial: Run Code Concurrently Using the Threading Module. Retrieved December 2019, from https://www.youtube.com/watch?v=IEEhzQoKtQU.

Rodriguez, I. (2019, April 4). What Is Pip? A Guide for New Pythonistas. Retrieved December 2019, from https://realpython.com/what-is-pip/.

Pipenv & Virtual Environments - The Hitchhiker's Guide to Python. (n.d.). Retrieved December 2019, from https://docs.python-guide.org/dev/virtualenvs/.

Pillow, Tutorial¶. (n.d.). Retrieved December 2019, from https://pillow.readthedocs.io/en/3.0.x/handbook/tutorial.html.

Schafer, C. (2017, October). Python Tutorial: re Module - How to Write and Match Regular Expressions (Regex). Retrieved December 2019, from https://www.youtube.com/watch?v=K8L6KVGG-7o.

SQLite Python: Creating a New Database. (n.d.). Retrieved January 2020, from https://www.sqlitetutorial.net/sqlite-python/creating-database/.

Lofaro, L. (2019, April 19). Working With JSON Data in Python. Retrieved January 6, 2020, from https://realpython.com/python-json/

Kinsley, H. (2014, July 18). Python 3 Programming Tutorial - Sys Module. Retrieved January 6, 2020, from https://www.youtube.com/watch?v=rLG7Tz6db0w

Chitipothu, A. (2019). 5. Iterators & Generators¶. Retrieved January 6, 2020, from https://anandology.com/python-practice-book/iterators.html

Weber, B. (2019, June 18). Defining Main Functions in Python. Retrieved January 6, 2020, from https://realpython.com/python-main-function/

Pryke, B. (2019, September 11). Jupyter Notebook for Beginners Tutorial. Retrieved January 8, 2020, from https://www.dataquest.io/blog/jupyter-notebook-tutorial/

Schafer, C. (2017, August 16). Python Tutorial: Unit Testing Your Code with the unittest Module. Retrieved January 8, 2020, from https://www.youtube.com/watch?v=6tNS--WetLI

Galli, K. (2019, February 1). Ad in 5 53:38 / 1:05:13 How to Program a GUI Application (with Python Tkinter). Retrieved January 14, 2020, from https://www.youtube.com/watch?v=D8-snVfekto

Sharma, A. (2019, December 10). (Tutorial) Introduction to GUI With TKINTER in PYTHON. Retrieved January 12, 2020, from https://www.datacamp.com/community/tutorials/gui-tkinter-python

Made in United States
Troutdale, OR
11/01/2024

24342872R00097